READ
TEACH!

5-minute motivators guaranteed to make kids want to learn

Kathy Paterson

Pembroke Publishers Limited

To my Mother,
who should have been a teacher

© 1994 Pembroke Publishers Limited
538 Hood Road
Markham, Ontario L3R 3K9

Canadian Cataloguing in Publication Data

Paterson, Kathleen M.
 Ready...set...teach!: 5-minute motivators
guaranteed to make kids want to learn

Includes index.
ISBN 1-55138-023-4

1. Teaching. 2. Motivation in education. I. Title.

LB1025.3.P37 1994   371.1'02   C94-930142-6

Editor: Kate Revington
Design: John Zehethofer
Cover Photography: Ajay Photographics
Typesetting: Jay Tee Graphics Ltd.

Printed and bound in Canada
9 8 7 6 5 4 3 2 1

Contents

Introduction

Motivation: reaction as a result of desire; that which acts as a spur to action

Webster's II New Riverside Dictionary

Motivation, or the lack thereof, is the key to learning. This idea is not any great revelation to teachers, but the creation of this elusive power remains, all too often, a mystery!

Although you may have the best intentions and teaching skills in the world, if the students are not in the right mental "set" for learning, your words will fall like seeds on barren soil. As a result, not only will minimal learning occur, but maximum behavioral management will be demanded of you. Uninterested students are restless students—no matter what the age group. But how, when children are raised with computers, video games, and stereo TVs, can a teacher interest students in such mundane activities as class work and books? Doing so is no easy task. Besides that, we tend to have so many facts stored in our heads that access to the wonderful motivational devices we may have been exposed to is almost impossible. How often I have said to myself, after a lesson, "...if only I had started that lesson with...." Hindsight! Afterthoughts! If onlys! *Too late!*

Ready...Set...Teach! brings to the fore the issue of warming up students to learn, that is, of motivating them through **anticipatory sets**. The term **set** is not meant to be jargonish or confusing; it is

5

meant to encompass all that is involved in beginning a lesson with pizzazz. Perhaps it can be thought of in this way:

<u>S</u>pontaneous <u>E</u>xciting <u>T</u>eaching

I have provided a compendium of attention-getting **sets**, which can be easily used before lessons in nearly all curriculum areas to focus students' attention on *you*—the teacher! These suggestions and ideas would also be useful to the substitute teacher who has the onerous task of quickly gaining students' attention and rapidly establishing rapport—an instant set could be a life saver in such a situation. Although my ideas may not be new—what ideas are?—perhaps all of us need a gentle reminding of everything available to us.

So read on—get ready, get **set**, and teach successfully!

Chapter 1: Setting the Lesson

Good teaching is one-fourth preparation and three-fourths theatre.

Sonia, a charismatic English professor,
in Gail Godwin's The Odd Woman

Why Use Sets?

My plans were made, all bright and new,
I'd worked them over—read them through—
This lesson would be something great!
To teach it I could hardly wait!
But there was something I forgot—
I was ready—my class was *not*!
Before me bodies formed a mass,
A restless lump that was my class.

Sara was braiding Jenny's hair,
Cory was chasing dreams somewhere—
Jessie's head was on her arms,
Willie was showing off his charms
To nearby girls all in a daze,
Giggling and whispering at Willie's ways
Brad was creating pencil "horns,"
While Sue was off with the unicorns,
Chris was thinking of basketball,
And Joey wasn't there at all!...

K. Paterson

Faced with such a daunting situation, it is easy to throw up your arms in dismay. But this is when your students need you most. You must put aside your lesson plans and get ready and set to motivate. Without that change of direction, you have no hope of focusing your students' attention on you.

This idea is borne out by a little survey I did of students from Grades 1 to 8. I asked some of them, "What makes a good teacher?" Although the answers varied, and statistically my survey was far from valid, a common theme emerged. Here are a few of the responses:

- Someone who loves us and gives us stuff. (Grade 1)
- Likes kids, and is nice and funny. (Grade 2)
- Someone who makes me laugh. (Grade 3)
- Someone who is happy and has a sense of humor. (Grade 4)
- Someone who makes me want to come to school. (Grade 5)
- Someone who at least tries to make the boring stuff less boring. (Grade 6)
- Someone with a good sense of humor and who can laugh with us. (Grade 7)
- Someone who makes us want to learn. (Grade 7)
- Someone who makes learning fun. (Grade 8)

I think the message is clear. Students seem to evaluate their teachers not so much on teaching skills, knowledge or ability to maintain order, but on their ability to engage students' attention—appealing to the students' sense of humor or empathizing with them is a way of doing this. So let us actively try to capture students' attention. Here are three actions, as defined in *Webster's New Collegiate Dictionary*, that I feel work together to help us to meet this goal:

- TEACH: to cause to know how; to guide the public; to instruct by example or experience; to seek to make known or accepted.
- ACT: to perform a specialized function for the public; to produce an effect through example; to represent, in a dramatic way.
- ENTERTAIN: to divert, direct or engage the public in such a manner that it will be both enjoyable and memorable to them.

As you can see, a distinct relationship exists between these three terms. Each pertains to the provision of a product or effect for the public in such a way that this product will be accepted. I suggest that teaching, good teaching, must, of necessity, call for all three actions: teaching, acting and entertaining. In addition, based on my own experiences, I can confirm that the chapter's introductory quotation by novelist Gail Godwin that teaching is three-fourths theatre is true. Even when an audience has been captured, the transmission of the actual lesson still puts the teacher in the role of an actor whose goal is to convey specific information, thoughts, feelings, or ideas to the audience. Thus the teacher becomes an entertainer, someone whose vocation includes providing sets to focus attention for what is to come. Just as we focus a camera to take a clear picture, we must focus students' minds so that they will have a clear imprint of a lesson.

Before a teacher can do this, however, the *teacher* must be motivated, focused, and prepared to entertain. Achieving this is not always easy, but is not impossible. We have all had "those days" when everything seemed to go wrong. Hindsight may reveal that either the tools of the entertainer (the sets) were ineffective or absent, or that they did not even excite the entertainer. Nothing great is ever achieved without enthusiasm. The teacher has to generate that enthusiasm and it will come only if he or she believes in the great importance of the teaching role. What hunger is to food, enthusiasm is to teaching! Again, you must be an actor, especially on days when you feel like crying; the moment you enter that classroom, you must assume the demeanor of one who is excited about what is to come. You can do this, because you are a teacher!

Warming Up to Learning

I entered my class on a bright Monday morning, my teaching batteries recharged over the weekend. I felt eager to begin teaching a new Math unit on geometry...my favorite! Then I looked over the sea of Grade 7 faces before me, and my heart sank! Jenny was asleep, head on her desk; Joe and Andy were arguing over a hockey game played the night before; Sharon was squeezing into the same desk as her new boyfriend; Dale was gazing out the window, chasing rainbows somewhere else—and not one student had a math book out or looked at all eager to pursue geometry! It did not take much effort to realize that these students, these "normal" young people, would have preferred to be almost anywhere else but in my Math class! Maybe Monday would not be such a great day after all...

The above scene, probably common to all teachers, was ripe for an anticipatory set, a motivational device to instill in the students, even if only for a short time, the desire to listen to what I had to say. Without it, most of the class would have left without even realizing that a new unit on geometry had begun. Unfortunately, I had *not* prepared a specific set for this lesson, and many of the students did leave the class with no more knowledge of geometry than when they came in. Fortunately, however, I came prepared the next day with a bag full of different items from home, a cylindrical coffee tin, a cube-shaped container and an oval mirror among them— each had some relationship to geometry. That lesson was a huge success.

I may have been unaware of the importance of a set for that first geometry class, but I had not been lazy. Teachers are always busy and cannot create motivational devices for every class. "Nor should they have to," some will say. "A teacher is there to teach, not entertain!" Since I only partly agree, let us consider this controversial topic more closely.

- Students will not learn unless motivated to do so.
- As a rule, students today lack an innate motivation to learn. Certainly, that has been my experience.
- Warming up before any activity, whether physical or mental, is important.
- Students understand and accept the need for warming up muscles before a physical activity; they tend not to understand that thinking requires a warm-up or opportunity to focus, too.
- Teachers must assume the responsibility of at least *attempting* to instill motivation before the teaching of a lesson.
- Although they might not believe it, teachers *are* entertainers who have the ability, if not the time, to create lesson-focusing sets.
- If sets are omitted from the lesson, the learning cycle is probably ineffective for teachers and students alike.

In a time so tuned-in to fitness and athletics, the learning process of students can be compared to a sport. First comes the warm-up which warns the muscles of action ahead! Next comes the activity, involving the now-ready muscles. And finally, there is the "cool down," or period of relaxation and reflection on the activity. Thus it is with learning. Students need to be warmed up (focused, alerted to what is to come, brain cells energized); taught (involved in the activity itself), and cooled down, (given time to review and reflect upon what has been presented). Too frequently, educators forget the first and last stages and concentrate only on the middle—the lesson-teaching stage! Experience has taught me that students not only are easier to manage but that they learn and retain more, if the other two steps are planned for and implemented.

Entrepreneur Henry Ford once said, "Coming together is a beginning; keeping together is progress; working together is success." His statement can be applied to the dynamics necessary in teaching. The "beginning" is the set; the "progress" is the lesson itself; the "success" is the close, or conclusion. All three must function together to form a complete whole.

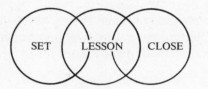

The lesson, if it stands alone, resembles the core of an apple—most of its flesh is gone; so too the set and close are gone.

Although the final step, that of concluding the lesson, will be examined in Chapter 9, as you will have gathered, this book focuses on ways in which we can overcome students' initial lack of motivation through warm-ups. I can assure you that no matter how exciting your lesson might be or how great the assignment it can fail if you do not start it off with flair and excitement, that is, with a prepared anticipatory set. If you enter the class and mutter, "Today we are going to learn about the use of fire in primitive societies by setting fire to our classroom," the students, most of them anyway, will have tuned out by your third word. You will not even get a reaction to your proposed insane suggestion. I have tried this, and found it to be true. On the other hand, if you walk in, place a foil plate on your desk, crumple a piece of paper on it and set fire to it, I guarantee you will have everyone's attention immediately! You have made them hungry to see what is going to happen next, and only hungry minds can become educated!

Now before you all jump up in protest saying that you cannot possibly carry on such a charade before every lesson—stop! Of course you can't, and that is not what I am suggesting. But a good set once a day, or every other day, or even less often if you find this type of activity particularly difficult (it gets easier with time, honest!) will do wonders for your overall teaching presence. The students will be more curious about what you might come up with next, and when! They will become more attuned to your lesson beginnings because they will not want to miss anything, and so when you *do* resort to the good old "Open your book to page 45" (yes, this, too, is a set, albeit an ineffective, boring one), they will be more likely to do as you ask. They will know that soon you will spark their interests again!

The Set Model

Let us consider what constitutes a good set before referring to anticipatory sets any further. Several criteria, at least some of which a set must meet, are outlined below and on page 13.

Criteria for Sets

1. *The set should focus attention on the material to be covered.*
   For example, when I sought to introduce my students to geometry by bringing in objects of different shapes, students participated in the hands-on activity of describing the shapes in geometric terms while I recorded the terms. The students were amazed to discover that everything can be broken down into a few basic shapes. Be sure to point out to students exactly how the set leads to the lesson at hand. (Specific explanations will follow many of the sets outlined in this book.)

2. *It should be relevant to the interests of as many of the students as possible.*
   For example, showing a cartoon from *The Far Side* will have far more effect on Junior High students than it will on young children. Be aware of the interests of your class as a whole.

3. *It should be brief and to the point.*
   A set that takes longer than about five minutes is taking away from teaching time more than it is facilitating teaching. A set is not a waste of time!

4. *It should make use of as many stimuli as possible.*
   Be visual, auditory and even tactile.

---

5. *It should enhance the learning experience.*
   A set should never become more important than the lesson itself. It does not replace the lesson.

6. *You may recall events that the class has shared* (eg., a trip to the zoo) *or create a common experience* (eg., bring a pet to the room).

7. *You may draw on your personal experiences.*
   Students love to hear about The Teacher. For example, to set the mood for writing about humorous events, I once described one of my most embarrassing moments: while I was wearing a brown paper bag over my head to set a lesson, the principal arrived unexpectedly in my classroom— to this day, that principal refers to me as the "Unknown Teacher."

8. *The set should require a response.*
   The response can be as simple as a raised hand or yes/no answer from all the students. For example: "How many of you have ever...?"

9. *It should be considered a part of the lesson.*
   Be sure to account for it when planning.

10. *Be sure to surprise the students.*
    Do not forewarn the students about what you are going to do. Just do it, allowing them to wonder and attend. Follow up the set with a reason for what you have done. In many of the suggested sets, the reasons are included. A few good openers to use before you dive into your set are as follows:

    Watch!
    Eyes here!
    Look at me now!
    Silence! Now, watch!
    This is a game!
    Listen quietly!

    Often no words are necessary. You simply begin the set, and within a short time, all eyes will be on you, even if just to see if you have finally "lost it," to use the students' own phrase!

Consider the effectiveness of the following two scenarios, both making use of the same set, for a lesson on observation skills (SCIENCE):

1. The teacher announces to the class: "Today we are going to talk about observation skills, in particular, seeing how things are both the same and different. I'm going to cut up some fruits and we will look at them together. (continues to cut up fruits, talking as she does so)

2. The teacher says nothing! Instead she produces, with flair, a big knife, a cutting board, and some unusual fruits such as kiwi and mango. The teacher says only, "Watch closely! We will talk about what you see after!" She begins cutting...

Which set do you think is more likely to captivate the audience? I am sure you can see what I am getting at. The less said, the better, at least initially!

The Classroom as Stage

In the speech that follows the assertion chosen as this chapter's opening quotation, the character Sonia promotes the value of the old-fashioned classroom structure: students are in the "audience" and the teacher is "up front." "I make it my business to utilize that separation, and it hasn't seemed to be so unpopular around here," she concludes.

I have spent many years in the classroom experimenting with desk/student placement, trying the semi-circle, numerous small groups of desks facing together, the wide centre aisle style and tables-as-opposed-to-individual-desks structure among others, but I must admit to returning to orderly rows of desks. With this structure, a good teacher is in a physical position to command the attention of the class, in much the same way as an actor on stage attracts the attention of the audience. The variations I do still make are to move *my* desk to different parts of the room (so that at times I may be behind the students) or to have all the rows face in the same, but new direction. One class aptly named this pattern of desk turning my "seasonal approach": I tended to have desks turned away from the windows in spring and toward the windows in winter, when bleak whiteness would not appeal to eager eyes.

The teacher, like an actor, is someone upon whom it is hoped all eyes will be cast. When the teacher is standing before a seated class, with desks in rows, he or she has no choice but to perform as if on stage. Also, eye contact is easy to make. None of the students are behind the teacher or even at the edges of peripheral vision, students know exactly where their eyes are to be focused, and the teacher has considerable freedom of movement throughout the class. The clear division between teacher and students effectively sets the stage for stimulating sets. If student desks encircle the teacher or are in small groups, some students will have to twist in their chairs, particularly if the teacher is using mime. At any given moment, many of the students will be unable to see the teacher's face. And even the most well-disciplined students tend to veer off task when the teacher's back is toward them.

If we accept the idea that the teacher is an actor who performs instructive theatre on the classroom stage, and who should, therefore, be in full view at the front, then what are we to make of the trend of so many of today's schools not to have orderly rows of desks? I believe the change is the result of honest teacher efforts to deal with the apparent lack of student motivation. Concerned teachers are seeking every possible means to rekindle in their charges an interest in learning. They hope that, by altering the general configuration of the class, students will experience a sense of "newness" and excitement. Perhaps students do, temporarily, but I do not believe the short-lived benefits merit drastic shifts away from the "classroom as stage" concept of teaching. Also, I have found that in most cases, the more the class setup varies from that of the conventional class, the more off-task and inappropriate behavior is evident. Perhaps students need and desire a certain amount of more formal structure in their lives, after all, and the widely recognized conventional classroom may provide just this.

Adopting the conventional classroom structure, however, calls for greater responsibility on the part of the teacher. Once a classroom has been established as a sort of theatre with definite stage and audience areas, the teacher is *always* the actor and cannot slack off in this role. And with our captive audiences, we have a responsibility to provide effective, lesson-focusing sets as often as possible.

Competition and Challenge

Throughout this book considerable reference is made to the creation of a game format, to competition, or to challenge, as well as to winners and losers. Although I realize that, as teachers, we have been educated to believe that competitive situations are harmful to the child, and that, at all costs, we should be keeping our classrooms non-competitive, non-threatening and without the stigmas associated with winning or losing, and I agree completely with the non-threatening part, life without a little competition is not a reality; however, I am not suggesting all-out competition for marks and so on, but rather a little challenge during the set component of a lesson. Having a challenge encourages participation and sparks interest. And at this time, perhaps more than at any other, the teacher can control, at least to some degree, the winners and the losers, so that not always the same few shine. As you read on and familiarize yourself with some of the suggested sets, you will gain a better understanding of what I mean.

Life is not fair, and students know that! They do not expect everybody to be treated in the same manner. In fact, I think they are far more realistic than we tend to be about the competition of life! So do not ignore a set because the word "challenge" jumps out at you. Meet it with an open mind and at least give it a try. It may not be for you. What works for one, does not for another. Students, too, respond differently to different stimuli and that is what makes teaching such a challenge! (Oops! That word again!) But if at first you don't succeed, you are certainly not alone!

Rewards and Reinforcement

If you *do* try to use a set that involves a mini-competition, you may want to give rewards of some sort. The rewards need not be tangible, although, of course, these are the easiest to handle (e.g., edibles, pencils, and stickers). They can be such as the following:

- teacher time (a few minutes one to one)
- a bathroom break to be taken immediately
- the chance to choose where to work for that period (students may surprise you with their choices)
- a drink break to be taken immediately
- the privilege of handing out something (works with younger students only)
- a serious handshake and public congratulations
- a "come up and take a bow" (loved or hated, depending upon your particular students—*know your students*!
- a hug (where appropriate) and
- permission to work at your desk (works amazingly well at *all* ages!)

Receiving edibles is always a favorite with students. If you are against the giving of candies, you can always choose boxes of cereal, nuts, crackers, grapes and raisins. But there are individually wrapped candies, candy kisses, big chocolate chips and so on, particularly in the bulk department of grocery stores, so I just add candies to my regular grocery list!

Determining rewards for your class just takes a bit of imagination and knowledge of your students. As this book is not about post-activity reinforcers, but about pre-activity motivators, I will leave this topic to your personal judgment. However, be assured that prizes make any game used as a set more meaningful, and heighten student interest.

Sets in the Teaching Spectrum

To believe that we can force students to learn is folly. To think that we can pique their curiosity daily about topics in which they have no interest is equally foolish. Our job, therefore, is to establish patterns of arousing excitement, of focusing attention, of sustaining student attention—of creating and using sets for learning.

No subject is without the need for good sets, although some lend themselves more easily to the establishment of them. In the following chapters, attention has been given to the creation of sets for specific subject areas. Although subjects such as French, Art, Drama, Computer Literacy and Physical Education have not been included, they, too, would benefit from snappy sets. Underlying assumptions of *Ready...Set...Teach!* are that the sets outlined can be adapted as needed and that teachers can come up with wonderful, unique sets of their own once the concept of the set is grasped.

Perhaps, you think "setting" is not your style, or you find the act difficult; nonetheless, make a special effort to have an eye-catching, pizzazz-filled set at the outset of every new unit. Having one then will help you really capture students' interest and focus it totally on the unit ahead. Characteristics such as intelligence, patience, and having a sharp memory and a thick hide may mark the successful teacher, but using exciting sets as tools is important, too.

Checklist for Set Creation and Presentation

____ Does the set focus attention on the material to be covered?

____ Is the set relevant to the interests of many of the students?

____ Will the set take five minutes or less to do?

____ Can the set apply to several lessons?

____ Does the set introduce a new unit?

____ Does the set make use of visual stimuli?

____ Of auditory stimuli?

____ Of tactile stimuli?

____ Does the set appeal to at least two of the senses?

____ Does the set clearly relate to the lesson?

How? _____

____ Does the set draw on experiences the class has shared?

____ Will the set create a common experience for the class?

____ Does the set allow you to talk about yourself?

____ Is a response required of students?

What is it? _____

____ Will the set surprise students?

How? _____

____ Do students' desks all face the same direction?

____ Is the classroom set up so that all students can see your face at the same time?

____ Will students see the set as a game?

____ Is the offering of rewards appropriate? What will they be?

_____

____ Do you have the costume bits, props and any handouts you

need? What are they? _____

____ Are you enthusiastic about teaching the lesson—or are you ready to pretend to be?

Chapter 2: Sets for the Written Word

"When *I* use a word," Humpty Dumpty said, in a rather scornful tone, "it means just what I choose it to mean—neither more nor less."

"The question is," said Alice, "whether you *can* make words mean so many different things."

"The question is," said Humpty Dumpty, "which is to be master—that's all!"

Lewis Carroll, Through the Looking Glass

You might wonder why topics related to reading and writing even require sets; however, let me remind you that for more and more students, especially those who are dyslexic or partially dyslexic and who are being integrated into the educational mainstream, language arts activities are extremely difficult and not at all pleasurable. We, as teachers, enjoy reading, or surely we would have chosen a different profession, but we cannot assume that the same is true of our students. We must, therefore, provide motivational sets even for story reading.

You will note that two chapters relate to language arts, this one and Chapter 3, and that together they are considerably longer than those that follow. There are several reasons for this. Language arts is highly important. It is the one subject in which the skills learned are utilized in all other subjects, and language proficiency may have a big impact on success in those subjects. Those who are uncomfortable with language arts activities face barriers. For example, I know a young man who came to Canada from China as a child: in all areas *except* language arts, he appears to be brilliant, yet because of his weak communication skills, he has been consistently denied entry to the post-secondary career of his choice. It is easy to see why more school hours are allotted to the teaching of communication skills than to any other curriculum area.

The other core subject areas are often accompanied by kits or units of study which include set suggestions for specific lessons. Also, the visual stimulus of a bunsen burner, for example, serves as a natural set, even for students who cannot read; a page of words or a worksheet on punctuation cannot do the same.

Finally, due to the subjectivity of the language arts program, every teacher teaches it somewhat differently, even when the curriculum is the same. As a result, teachers' guides for language arts tend not to suggest sets. Goals and objectives may be concretely laid out, but the way in which they are to be met is usually left up to the Language Arts teacher. In an effort to help teachers generate sets for language arts, I have heavily weighted this area of set creation.

Reading

As a rule of thumb, a story to be read is introduced by a discussion of the title, its possible relevance to the story, what it might mean, and so on. I find this type of introduction very boring, as do students who have become so accustomed to it that they often do not focus at all. However, several equally quick and easy ways to introduce a story or manuscript to be read exist. The following sets are more interesting than the standard one but still not as stimulating as the final suggestions (which cannot be used *all* the time). Note that although I have suggested the type of story in each instance, the same ideas can be used with any theme or story.

Stimulating Sets

Introduce a story to be read by any of the following methods or combinations of methods.

- QUESTIONING TECHNIQUES (re: an animal story)
  1. "How many of you have a pet?"
  2. "Did any of you happen to watch the movie *Benji*?"
  3. "I have a dog and last night he...."
  4. "Remember when we visited the zoo? Think back to what the otters were doing..."

- SETTING THE SCENE (re: an adventure story)
  1. Have you ever been home alone, perhaps babysitting (age specific), and heard strange noises from somewhere in the house?"

2. "Imagine this: you are on a camp-out in the wilderness, no adults. You get totally lost, and it starts to storm...."
3. "Let's pretend we are in the Arctic. It's freezing cold and one of us gets caught on a ice floe...." (I once opened the windows in the middle of winter to set the atmosphere.)

   Note: Any of these scene setters will probably lead to much discussion which you can then steer to the story at hand.

- GIVING HINTS (re: a mystery story)
  1. "In most mystery or murder stories, who do people usually say "did it"?...(the butler). Is this always the case."
  2. "I'm going to give you a hint about someone in this class. You guess who it is. (eg., This person is probably getting less sleep these days. Joey...just got a new baby brother.) Hints are given in mystery stories, too. In this story...."
  3. "How do we differentiate between "good guys" and "bad guys"? Have you ever noticed that authors tend to describe the villains in certain ways? What if the author really wanted to fool you?"

     Note: Naturally the hints you use will depend entirely on the story.

- THE BEGINNING
  Before even asking students to get their books out, tell them what the story is about in such a way as to pique their curiosity. You might ask students to guess the story context from the title or to create mind pictures based on it. If the story is open-ended, you could invite students to tell you about something they thought had not ended properly. You could also tantalize them with a picture from the story.

More Stimulating Sets

- VISUAL STIMULI (re: an animal story)
  1. Bring a picture of animals or of the specific animal in the story. Collect posters so that you have a pool to draw on. Posters can be lifesavers!
  2. Bring a stuffed toy animal.
  3. Make an overhead transparency of one of the pictures that accompany the story, or, if the story has no illustrations, find one elsewhere.
  4. Bring the real thing! (Of course, doing this is practical only

in a few cases. Once when we read a wonderful horse story, I used a model of a horse rather than try to convince my principal of the merits of dragging a real horse into my classroom!)

- TACTILE STIMULI (re: an animal story)
  1. Bring a piece of fur and have students guess what kind of animal it has come from.
  2. Take students on a quick sensory image tour such as the following: "Close your eyes and imagine you are in a beautiful green forest. You feel peaceful and happy. You can feel the soft grass beneath you. Suddenly, you hear a rustle behind you, but you are not afraid. Then there is a gentle warm tongue licking at your hand and you feel the soft breath of a young animal beside you. Reach out and stroke the smooth, soft fur of the...."

  (re: a mystery story)
  3. "Close your eyes and imagine yourself in a creaky old house. Reach out and touch the cobwebs...feel the rough walls, reach down and touch the cold, damp floor...."

  (re: a desert or lost-at-sea type of story)
  4. Pass around a salt shaker and ask students to put a little salt in their hands and lick it. Then tell them they cannot have a drink. (Naturally you will provide water in a few minutes.) Discuss the desire for water. Letting students experience something central to the story is an excellent set.

- AUDITORY STIMULI
  1. *Tell* (do not read) the beginning of the story to the class. Begin by asking how many have had grandmothers or older siblings tell them stories. Then say you are going to tell them a story. Use lots of eye contact and exaggerated emotion. Then let students read the story to find out how it ends.
  2. Taped music playing at the beginning of class without any introduction by the teacher will arouse the curiosity of all. The music must, of course, lead to the story. For example, Glen Miller's "Baby Elephant Walk" before a circus story would be appropriate. Sound effects records, available at public libraries, also make wonderful story sets.

- BOX STIMULI
  Put together a box of props from which you can draw items at a moment's notice. Although these Box Items can be used in any subject area, I have chosen to introduce them here, and will refer

to them elsewhere in this book as the Box Items. They serve as simple sets in as many ways as your imagination will take you, for example, using an eye patch to launch a story about pirates. A list of key items appears on this page and the next.

Box Items

_____ Hats, all shapes and kinds

_____ Pins and badges, eg., a sheriff's badge, a police identification card, an army medal

_____ Tunics, sashes and swatches of colorful material that can be draped around oneself to create an instant foreigner, old person, Mexican...

_____ Toy weapons (available everywhere at Halloween)

_____ A variety of toys, dolls and stuffed animals

_____ A variety of old shoes of varying sizes

_____ Unusual pictures (eg., I have used a picture of a woman dressed in fashionable clothing while riding a horse backwards for everything from a lesson on fashion to one on humor to one on social mannerisms.)

_____ A flashlight (It is amazing what happens when lights are turned off and a flashlight is the only light source.)

_____ Balloons

_____ Party favors

_____ Shells

_____ Dried flowers

_____ Holiday souvenirs

_____ Candles and sparklers

_____ Incense

_____ Edibles with specific taste (salt, sour candies, sugar cubes, cinnamon sticks, licorice drops, mints, chocolate coffee beans)

_____ Samples of "smells" (perfume samples, ammonia, bleach, lemon juice, cocoa, spices)

_____ Old wigs

___ An old phone

___ A large key

___ A "talking stick" (Any piece of interesting-looking wood will do: mine is a miniature totem pole picked up at a souvenir shop. Only the person holding the stick may talk.)

___ Oversized glasses

___ Groucho Marx nose/moustache

___ A magic wand, such as can be purchased cheaply in novelty stores and toy departments

___ Magic dust (sparkle dust put into an old-looking salt shaker)

The contents of my Box are constantly changing and reflective of me. For example, I also use a huge pine cone from the Redwood Forest in California and a blue glass sphere which was once a fisherman's float. There is no limit to what you can hoard. It is how you use your resources that counts.

Most Stimulating Set

- STUDENTS AS PROTAGONISTS

  I save this set until June when patience and creativity are running on empty and spring fever has reached epidemic proportions. Write (don't panic...I'll help you) a story where all the students in your class are the protagonists! Students like nothing better, egocentric as they are, than to read about themselves. In theory, you can take any story and insert the names of your students, but I have found that most stories do not have enough characters. I therefore create my own stories, which I save on computer disk and reuse with different names year after year. By June you will readily know which of your students best fits each spot in the story. You will, however, have to take the time to insert the names appropriately even if you choose to adopt the story provided in Appendix A. Let me assure you though that the story can be used for several sequential classes to cover many aspects of comprehension, writing and grammar. This set, also an integral part of the lesson, is, without a doubt, my favorite Language Arts activity for the near-end of the year. And it must be so with the students too, because they rush to class to read the end of the story, or (if you are very diligent) the next chapter. Even reluctant readers enjoy the stories and often ask when they can have another special one to read. And alumni students have told me years later that they have kept and read the stories many times.

Writing

In many cases, the same sets used for reading can be used for writing, but here you are not limited by the content of the already written word. The key is: The more interested the students are in the set, the more likely they will be to write. In addition, the more specific the set, the more likely that students will write. In other words, asking students to write a descriptive paragraph about the bizarre collection of papers on your desk will not likely generate much of a response. Instead, try the first set suggested below, and compare the difference in results. A few other sets that have worked for me follow.

- THE STAGED HOLDUP: I bribed a fellow teacher to dress in a mask and old coat, rush into my classroom and wildly steal some papers from my desk. You can see the many ramifications of such a shared experience. The set could trigger lessons for Science ("What did you *really* see?"), Social Studies ("Why do people steal?"), Art (Draw the thief) or Mathematics ("How many papers were taken?). I chose to use it for writing. The students wrote wonderful accounts of the incident, all quite different. From this take-off, many other lessons followed.

- BUBBLES: Filling the air with beautiful bubbles seems to capture the attention of even the most reticent of writers, who will then try to write descriptions of the ethereal spheres. One student went so far as to write a wonderful story about life inside a bubble!

  Note: Here is an excellent recipe for huge bubbles...as big as a child's head: Mix 1 part JOY liquid detergent (for some reason it works the best), 1 part glycerine, 1 part water. Make huge bubble hoops by bending wire into circular shapes. Awesome!

- SHOES (or Hats/Coats/Scarfs...whatever): Arrange different types of shoes in front of the class and discuss what kinds of people may have worn each. Doing so promotes writing character analyses, short stories, or just simple descriptions of one shoe.

- MYSTERY ENVELOPE: A large brown envelope addressed to the class can serve as an interesting story-starter. The envelope can be kept sealed: "Write about its possible contents." It can contain an unusual invitation (see below) to which students must respond, or a photograph about which a story must be written. The possibilities are endless; the interest factor is the envelope itself.

SAMPLE INVITATION

> *Dear* _____:
> *You are cordially invited to the Spooks Anonymous costume party, to begin at midnight, in the old mansion at the end of Willow Lane.* (Use an actual address here.) *Please respond by informing us of what you plan to wear, what goodies you will provide, and what guest you will bring.*
> > *Hauntingly yours,*
> > *Lady Vampira*

- THE TEA PARTY: This set covers both language arts and social studies content, something that is appropriate with the push toward integration between subjects. You surprise your class with a little party, preferably with unusual food and drink, for example, mini tacos and punch while studying Mexico in Social Studies. Share the treats; discuss what it felt like to do this unexpected thing and assign a writing task. Allow students to write according to their abilities and interests: some may be capable only of a few good descriptive sentences, others may discuss their feelings and still others may want to write thank-you letters or complete stories.

Note: You might want to have your class brainstorm for a couple of lead sentences that can be left on the board to be copied or used in some form. Example: "One day our class was sharing fortune cookies when Carrie found the most unusual message in hers."

- THE PET ROCK: After you have established a Return to Room cue, have a five-minute scavenger hunt. Each student is to seek a small pebble or rock. If none are usually seen in the area, find some, bring them, and scatter them around as you would for a peanut scramble. In fact, you can use peanuts instead of rocks, but I find the students get more "involved" with rocks. Once each of them has found a rock, they must write about it: where it was found, why it was chosen, what it is called and what special powers it has.

Note: The older the students, the more complicated the writing can become, from a few descriptive sentences to a complete story about how The Rock saved the day...whatever!

- COLORS: When at a loss for an interesting topic that fits your current theme, try this. Scan the room for the most popular color being worn that day and ask all those who are wearing that color to stand. Doing this immediately grabs attention as students wonder what is going on. Then tell students something about what that color is associated with and ask if the association matches how they are feeling that day. For example, yellow can signify happiness and gaiety. Do the same with other colors until all students have had a chance to stand up. Then ask them to write about their favorite color, either using the information you have given them or making it up. Allow them to choose the genre in which they want to express their thoughts, for example, poetry or essay. Before students begin writing, have the class discuss such titles as "How Red Saved My Life," "Yellow Makes Me Happy," and "Blue is Beautiful" to help their minds focus further. Displaying posters that are predominantly one color adds much to this lesson. And creating a design or picture using only tints and shades of one color makes a great follow-up.

- MUSICALLY MINDED: Tell the students only that you want them to listen to a few songs and that they should pay particular attention to the words. Your choices are important because students will be expected to write the story suggested by a song. For example, "The Wall" by Pink Floyd, "The Unicorn" by the Irish Rovers, "Tom Dooley," a traditional song sung by the Kingston Trio, and "Imagine" by John Lennon are all strong candidates. You will want to play the songs more than once and discuss them. Once students begin writing, I make several cassette players with headphones available so that they can come and listen to the song of their choice again. I provide several copies of each song and have the words on handouts. Preparing for this lesson may seem quite demanding, but you can get a lot of mileage out of it. In addition to the writing assignment, you can invite groups to research the singer(s) and prepare reports to be presented orally; ask for illustrations to accompany the stories; assign the writing of sequels to the original stories; and encourage the creation of cartoon strips of the songs, which would require knowledge of main idea and sequencing. The replaying of the song(s) at the beginning of each lesson resets or refocuses the students to the task at hand.

- CREATING AN ATMOSPHERE: Have the lights off and curtains closed when students enter and assume a serious, quiet demeanor. Talk to them as if you are very scared and tell them you have something you wish to share with them. The dimness and lowered voice will capture their attention. Now it is up to you to be the actor— you can, because you *believe* you can!—And tell, in your most convincing manner, a story such as the following:

> Last night I decided to go for a walk at about midnight because I couldn't sleep, and the weirdest thing happened. I still don't know if it was real or imagined. I was walking close to (name an actual place to which the students can relate) when I heard my name being called...very quietly. It was dark. There was no moon, and I couldn't see anyone, so I kept walking. Then I heard it again. "Kathy...Kathy...." (Using your first name is more effective here.) I was scared by now so I started to run, but suddenly I heard the voice in front of me. Well, you can imagine how I felt then. I didn't know what to do. I called out, "Who's there? If this is a joke it's not funny!" But the voice just kept calling "Kathy... Kathy...." Then I saw what looked like a person dressed in a nightgown in front of me. I thought it was some lady lost or something so I started to move toward her until I realized she was standing...well, I guess "floating" would be a better word...about 1 m off the ground. That was enough for me. I turned and ran as fast as I could but she kept appearing in front of me, calling my name in the most pathetic way. I kept running anyway and as I got close to her, I closed my eyes and ran my hardest. Suddenly, I fell (show some bruise or make-up bruise or scratch) and as I did, I felt her clothing brush me. I've never been so terrified in my life. When I got home, I called the police to see if any more incidents like that had been reported and they thought I was crazy. But look (hold up a piece of white gauze) I ended up at home with this in my hand....

Stop at this point and allow for discussion. Some students will laugh and dismiss your story as fake, but depend upon your acting ability. As I've said many times before, teachers *are* actors.

Try to continue the charade for a few more moments, then turn on the lights and admit to the fraud. Then ask what made it convincing, how they felt when you were telling it, and so on. Be sure students see beyond the dark room and your voice tone. Brainstorm for some of the images you used: lack of moon, midnight, the floating of the spectre, the sudden appearance of the spectre. This set focuses attention on the importance of creating an atmosphere in a story and generally excites the students about writing their own stories. It is great at Halloween time, but is effective at any time and with any age. Just be careful not to really frighten young students.

- MOSTLY MAGIC: Dig into The Box and pull out your magic wand, magic powder, or magic sphere (blue glass float). Hold it silently in front of you until all eyes are on you, wondering what on earth you are going to do now. Then tell the students that through your magic, you will grant each of them one wish, but the wish must benefit humankind as well as the individual and it cannot be a wish for more wishes. Give them exactly one minute to think of a wish, then have each student share his or her wish. (This can be done in groups to save time.) Now discuss the many possible dangers of getting what we wish for, particularly if you have older students. Then go around granting each student his or her wish by tapping with the wand, placing hands on the sphere, or sprinkling with a little sparkle dust. Next step, provide a few starter sentences on the board, which can be used by the students if they want to, and have them write about what happened when they made their wishes.

- THE KEY: Again, dig into The Box and take out your huge, old key. (If you do not have one, any key will do, but the bigger the better.) Stand in front of the class and pretend to be examining the key very closely. Before long, students will ask questions and want to see the key too. Tell them this key is special because it can open doors that no other key can, doors to the future, to the past, to people's minds, to magic kingdoms, et cetera. Limit the doors according to the age and type of students; very young students, for example, would not be able to handle the idea of opening doors to people's hearts, or minds, while Junior High students would love this idea. Discuss some of the possibilities of owning such a key. Then discuss the assignment. It does not have to be a story, but can be any type of writing you choose. A comparison between two divergent worlds (one visited with the key), a character analysis (after opening the door to the heart of a famous person), a few descriptive sentences (after opening the door to one's soul), and a report (after opening the door to the future) are all possibilities. It is the seeing and touching of the key that focuses, or sets, the students. Be sure that each student can handle the key to open whatever he or she wishes to.

- STORY PARTS: When teaching the parts of a story, a great attention catcher is to say, "I can tell you the shortest story in the world." Then say (and write):

The last man on earth heard a knock at the door.

The students will be amazed that this sentence contains all the components of a short story. Try it and you will be surprised, too!

- FUN WITH PHRASES: Without saying a word, either have the lights off when students enter the room, or turn them off and have an age-appropriate saying written boldly (preferably in color) on the overhead, which is more effective than the chalkboard. An example is this quotation by Mark Twain:

"Don't let schooling interfere with education."

Or, this one by Walter Winchell:

"A real friend is one who walks in when others walk out."

Allow the students a few minutes to ponder the expression, then discuss it, and any others the students themselves come up with. Assign an opinion paragraph or essay, or even a short story, based on a similar epitaph. Some of my favorite sources are *Think Again* by Dr. Robert Anthony (Berkley Books) and *More Jokes for Children* by Marguerite Kohl and Frederica Young (Farrar, Straus & Giroux).

- CANDLELIGHT DELIGHT: Turn off the lights and begin lighting one candle for each desk. The inexpensive, squat candles used for warming dishes are the safest, but any candles, even birthday cake ones, will do. After lighting all the candles and asking for absolute quiet, produce a rolled-up piece of paper on which you have written a message (see below). To make the paper look "authentic," you can crumple it before rolling, tear or burn the edges, or even splurge on a piece of rice or parchment paper. Tell the students you found this scroll in your attic (here comes that acting ability again) and want to share its message with them. After you have done so and they have realized the hoax, discuss how the candlelight and so on helped to "set the stage." Then the students must write similar messages and make them appear old. You will be surprised at how creative they can be. They must hand in their messages rolled up and tied somehow. Allow them to write by the candlelight for a while to stimulate their creative juices. Just be sure to have water on hand. You might need it...

SAMPLE MESSAGE

Dear Friend:
I have been trapped in this cave for many years...more years than I can count. My beard has grown to my knees and my eyes have become weak. At first I thought I would become insane, but the loneliness has become my friend. This huge cave has been my home since the cave-in that killed my partner so long ago. I have given up all hope of rescue, but in case my bones are ever found, I want it known that I loved my wife, Betty, till the day I died. And please tell her

• EPITAPHS: Although not appropriate for Grades 1 to 4, this set is enjoyed by older students, who treat it lightheartedly. Of course, as with anything a teacher does, be sensitive to the specific students in the class, and never introduce an activity that might cause grief or discomfort, in this case, reminder of a recent death in the family. As a set, have a tombstone drawn on the board, or, better still, on the overhead. Show an epitaph, such as "Lived as he died—loved by all," and discuss this. Then offer a few epitaphs, such as these which were suggested by the persons mentioned:

W.C. Fields: "On the whole, I'd rather be in Philadelphia."
Actor Wallace Ford: "At last I get top billing!"
Actress Dorothy Lamarr: "This is too deep for me."

This exercise can promote the development of concisely expressed main ideas or can encourage students to see and use dual word meanings. I used it before an exercise on the incorrect use of sentence run-ons, something at which most students seem to be very good. It worked well!

- OBITUARIES: Begin the class with the solemn reading of several obituaries from the newspaper. Then discuss the meaning and importance of these, and what students would like to have said about themselves. Let them be creative. They can write obituaries for the present, or for sometime in the future after they have become famous! I shall never forget one quiet, unobtrusive little chap in Grade 6 who astonished us all with a wonderful obituary about himself as a world-famous rock star with millions of fans and several wives. Needless to say, his image in the class changed somewhat after this assignment.

- DEAR ABBY: Begin the class with the following statement clearly visible on the overhead or chalkboard:

  I've been reading advice columns for years, and the way I figure it, the happiest man in the world must be "Mr. Abby."

Before discussing the joke, play the song, "Dear Abby" by John Prine. By now curiosity will be aroused. Pass around several copies of Dear Abby letters from a newspaper and allow a few minutes for comparison and discussion. Then assign students to be Abby and write logical answers to problems. You can brainstorm together for several problems (limit the number and set a word limit for the replies), or you can simply put a few of your own suggestions on the board and allow students to choose one or two. Here is an example.

  My dog keeps eating my homework, but my teachers think I am lying about it...
  Signed, Truth Teller

Of course, you can split the class into two parts: one side writing the letters, the other answering, and vice versa. This fun activity not only encourages creativity, but good writing skills, because a published column such as Dear Abby should be polished.

Reading and writing are such critically important skills that we must do all we can to ensure that our students are turned on to these rewarding activities. With illiteracy such a potent threat to future well-being and prosperity, we must use all our resources and imagination to help students focus on reading and writing—and learn! Creating effective sets should play an invaluable role in helping us to realize our goals.

Chapter 3: ... for the Spoken and Unspoken Word

> "Then you should say what you mean," the
> March Hare went on.
> "I do," Alice hastily replied; "at least—at least
> I mean what I say—that's the same thing you
> know."
> "Not the same thing a bit!" said the Hatter.
> "Why, you might as well say that 'I see what I
> eat' is the same thing as 'I eat what I see'!"
>
> *Lewis Carroll, Alice's Adventures in Wonderland*

Grammar

Some of us may not even want to teach grammar or perhaps think
we do not need to, but, like listening and speaking skills with which
it is grouped in this chapter, grammar is something students need
to know. Specific questions come to mind. Do students not learn
grammar by osmosis? Is it not wrong to teach grammar rules in
isolation? Will isolated grammar facts hold true for all communi-
cations? I do not have the answers to these age-old questions. All
I know is that in my more than 16 years of teaching, the spiral of
"to teach or not to teach grammar" continues to go around and
around.

I suggest that if you do decide to teach tenses, nouns, verbs, punctuation, et cetera, to students who usually find this boring, do it
with flair. I, myself, enjoy teaching grammar and respect its very
preciseness; often, my own excitement for the subject helps students
to get more out of it. If, however, you are unenthusiastic about
the passing on of grammar skills, there are still ways to teach it
effectively. Recall that in Chapter 1 I said teachers are actors—
when it comes to teaching grammar, this may be a time to perform!
Think positively! Remember that your personal biases will reflect

in your teaching, and will affect the students' learning. So begin by convincing yourself that grammar is important and that you might as well teach it as effectively as possible, with the help of a few good sets. In this section I offer a few suggestions on spicing up and focusing attention on some of the most common grammar areas.

- PUNCTUATION: Write several sentences that are open to misinterpretation on the chalkboard or overhead before the students enter. Say nothing other than "Please follow the directions." Here is a good example of unpunctuated sentences: *While sitting in your desk quickly write your name on the back side of the paper fold it in half.* Let students ponder possible understandings for a while, then add appropriate punctuation. Your point will be well made. (While sitting in your desk, quickly write your name on the back side of your paper. Fold it in half.) The same idea can be applied to a piece of dialogue, such as the following split quotation: *Come in Mary said Bill I need your help.*

- PARTS OF SPEECH: Ask the students to supply you with names of things (nouns). List several, such as desk, boy, pencils and books, on the chalkboard, write a sentence missing the noun, and add their choices. For example: We were so hungry we all ate _____ for lunch! The same thing can be done with other parts of speech. Make a list of fill-ins and save them. You can actually take an entire paragraph, remove words of your choice, ask for student input, then add student words to the paragraph. Sometimes the results are hilarious.

SAMPLE PARAGRAPH AND LIST OF PARTS OF SPEECH

One __*1*__ day our class was feeling __*2*__ so we decided to __*3*__. We packed __*4*__ and __*5*__ for lunch and set off into the woods. We played games such as __*6*__ and __*7*__. Then (*name of class member*) took out a huge wad of bubble gum which got stuck to a __*8*__. We all tried to __*9*__ it off. Then (*name of class member*) __*10*__ it. Finally we were __*11*__ so we __*12*__ home __*13*__.

1. adjective	6. noun	11. adverb
2. adjective (emotion)	7. noun	12. verb(ed)
3. verb	8. noun	13. adverb
4. noun(s)	9. verb	
5. noun(s)	10. verb(ed)	

See Appendix B, "Playing with Parts of Speech," for more samples.

- PLURALS: Have the following on the overhead: (Your name) said, *"Correct this sentence, (Student's name). The bull and the cow is in the field."* (Student) said, *"The cow and the bull is in the field. Ladies always come first!"* Discuss! Enjoy! Use as a set for a lesson on plural verbs.

- PRONOUN USAGE: Write the following on the overhead: (Your name) asked, *"Please correct this sentence, (student's name): It was me who broke that window."* (Student) answered: *It was **not** me who broke that window!"* Again, discuss! Enjoy! Use as a set for a lesson on pronouns.

Word Usage

- CONNOTATION/DENOTATION: Although you may not wish to introduce the words "connotation" and "denotation" to your class, pointing out subtle differences in words students use is often necessary, especially when students are describing characters. For example, one student once referred to his protagonist as a "wimpy, smart guy"; what he really meant was "slender, smart guy." Here is an effective set. Tell students as briefly as possible to brainstorm for all the words that mean "unattractive." They will soon fill the board with everything from "ugly" to "grotesque" to words I am sure you have never even heard of. If they do not have any words of milder connotations, for example, "plain" and "homely," add some, or encourage them to get some. Then comes the fun part. Tell them the following story.

> You are standing in the hall: your teacher is behind you, and a friend is beside you. At the other end of the hall are several women, all dressed alike, and with the same color of hair. Your friend knows that one of them is your teacher's wife, but doesn't know which one, and asks you. Your teacher's wife is quite ugly. If you had to, how could you convey this to your friend when you know your teacher can hear you.

Insist that students deal with the appearance issue so that connotation/denotation differences will quickly become clear to them. I have used this set successfully with Junior High students, choosing the word "overweight" (I was sure no overweight students were in that particular class). The students got so excited about it, that they wanted to find other words with which to repeat the exercise. They came up with the following words with negative connotations such as you need for this exercise: unintelligent, over talkative, sloppy, clumsy, and vain.

Note: When using this particular set, be sure to note that appearance is only one small part of a person and not necessarily a reliable basis on which to judge someone. Students are generally already aware of this.

- ALPHABET GAME: This set brings home to students that they must know alphabetical order before attempting to use a thesaurus or dictionary. Tell the students that they are going to play a game (there's that attention-getting word again!). Every sentence or phrase they say is to begin with the next letter of the alphabet—in sequence. Doing this takes a little practice, but can have hilarious results. Begin by giving the students a "setting," for example, a zoo.

STUDENT 1: <u>A</u>h, what a lovely day!
STUDENT 2: <u>B</u>oy, this is going to be fun at the zoo!
STUDENT 3: <u>C</u>an you believe we actually skipped school to come here?

- FUN WITH WORDS: Start off by saying, "I'll bet you guys (my word again) didn't know that words can be fun! We are going to find out right now what I mean. Take the word 'lazy,' for instance. What does it mean?" Students will give you a variety of appropriate answers. Accept them, but then explain that you want them to be creative and to think up other ways to explain the word. For example: Lazy is someone who steps into a revolving door and waits, or lazy is someone who has sworn never to work on any week that has a Tuesday in it. Once they get the idea, students do this activity marvellously well and begin to think about words in general, a good focus for whatever you want to teach about words, vocabulary, prefixes, suffixes, even spelling! Here are some words that have worked for me: ugly, depressed, silly, snob, hyperactive and teacher (but do not use this word unless you feel open-minded and secure that day!).

Perhaps more than any other area of language arts, grammar is full of rules. But within those confines, you can still introduce aspects of the subject creatively and even provide your students with fun.

Listening

This component of language arts is often overlooked or dealt with in a somewhat off-hand manner. All of us are all guilty! But students need to be taught and retaught to listen effectively, and then given plenty of practice to refine this important skill. The following anticipatory sets could precede any listening lesson. Key focusing phrases follow each suggestion.

- STORYTELLING: Once, when I was taking a Childrens' Literature class at university, the professor came in, story book in hand, and sat on the front of her desk, facing us. She opened the book, but instead of reading the story to us, she *told* it...word for word...even down to the little meaningless phrases such as "to be sure," and "of course." As she completed each page (the book was facing us—she couldn't see it at all), she would turn the page at exactly the correct time, and continue as if she were reading it. And all the time she maintained complete eye contact with us. We were mesmerized. Had the story, which was really rather silly, been Shakespeare's *Macbeth*, we would have been no more impressed. If the telling of a child's story could have such an impact on adults, think of the impact storytelling could have on students. I have tried telling stories, and it works! The students, just as we were, are astounded that you have memorized the entire book. And it is not difficult to do. Children's stories are simple, and if you miss or change a word or two, no one will be the wiser. But the impact is terrific!

  Afterwards, you can discuss good listening skills with them, exploring such issues as why they were more apt to listen to the story and how they can use those listening techniques elsewhere.

- NO WORDS: Without any explanation, show a few minutes of an action-packed video, without any sound. Ignore requests to turn up the sound. Complete this set with a discussion of the importance of sound. Discuss (or write on chart paper, using the whole language or total class approach) what students think was being said, then review, this time with the sound.

- WHAT DID YOU SAY?: If the issue of deafness is handled properly, students can appreciate that it is OK to enjoy the humor created by elderly persons having a conversation subject to constant misinterpretation. Begin by asking how many students have grandparents who have difficulty hearing. Then have partners prepare brief conversations as if they were two elders. Give an example such as this:

  A: Ain't it a great day?
  B: No, I don't want to play!
  A: What? You saw a play? What was it about?
  B: Shout! I didn't shout!

To keep this activity within the confines of a set, allow no more than five minutes for partners to try this, and choose only one pair to demonstrate for the class. You can then focus the class on listening by commenting that what we actually hear is very important and can make a big difference to our lives.

- TELEPHONE: Tell the students they are going to play a game. Whisper a simple sentence at one side of the room, and let it be passed on all around the room until it reaches the other side. Naturally, the final version will be different from the initial sentence. Focus attention on the reason for this activity by saying that legends and stories are passed through the ages in a similar way; also, rumors grow dangerous by being passed on by word of mouth. You are now ready for another lesson in listening.

- LISTEN TO THE SILENCE: Without explanation, ask all students to begin tapping their fingertips on their desks as loudly as they can, but to make no other noise except this for one full minute. Then signal them to stop and be silent. The silence will seem ominous and overwhelming. Discuss this, as well as background noise. (What could you hear? Do we always hear these things or do we block them out? Do we sometimes block out voices too?) Repeat the exercise, this time asking students to listen to their own hearts during the silence. Students find it amazing that the room can be so silent in this great set for any listening lesson. And remember to whisper as low as you can when you break the silence to show them that they can, in truth, hear what you are whispering. Very powerful!

- SOUND EFFECTS: After introducing this set as a game, give each student (or pair) a sheet of paper. Have them identify as many sounds on a sound effects record (available at any music store) as you wish to use. Doing so will provide a great set for a lesson in listening.

- JUST FOR FUN: Allow students to listen to something just for the fun of it. Younger students love silly, funny stories, but they also enjoy Stephen Cosgrove's Serendipity Books. A wonderful, totally ridiculous book that is thoroughly enjoyed by even the most difficult-to-reach Junior High student is Roald Dahl's *Revolting Rhymes* (Puffin Books). Actually, any of Roald Dahl's books by Puffin are excellent listening-for-pleasure books. Other "fun" books include limerick, riddle, and verse books such as *The Great All-time Excuse Book* by Maureen Kushner (Sterling Publishing), *Giggles, Gags & Groaners* by Joseph Rosenbloom (Sterling Publishing), *The Craziest Riddle Book in the World* by Lori Miller Fox (Sterling Publishing), and *The Armada Lion Book of Young Verse* edited by Julia Watson (Collins).

Speaking

Another often overlooked component of Language Arts is speaking skills. For many students, public speaking seems to come quite naturally, but to others, it is terrifying. In this area, above all others, teacher empathy is a must! Remember that although public speaking is probably a mandated component of your language arts curriculum, not everyone of us is going to need this skill in life, and as long as we can communicate in other situations, such as one to one, perhaps standing in front of a class and giving a speech to peers is unnecessary. I say this because I once had a timid young girl faint from the fear of having to give an oral presentation and never recover from the humiliation. Never again will I force a student to speak in front of a class. Teacher modelling of good public speaking techniques may be all that you do.

However, given that teachers think their students would benefit from the development of this skill and are expected to promote effective public speaking within the language arts curriculum, sets are available.

- MUCH ADO ABOUT NOTHING: Enter your class dressed "differently." By this I mean, look into The Box and come up with something...anything...a hat, glasses, an overcoat...whatever. Add a pointer or cane if available. Use a podium where one is available. Perhaps use a briefcase too. Change the manner in which you walk and stand. Assume the demeanor of some important character, and firmly announce to the class that they are to listen to your words of great insight. Your change will be enough to trap their attention. Then you must deliver, in your most pontificating manner, a short speech about something totally insignificant. Doing so will point out that not just the content of the speech matters, but also the way in which the speech is delivered. In addition, this technique will interest the students in trying to deliver such a speech themselves. The following short speech, although lacking the impact of delivery, should inspire you to create a similar speech on another such insignificant topic as "Why Humpty *Really* Fell off the Wall!" or "The Importance of Saying Please and Thank You." Your set is actually a model for the assignment you will give to your students.

> I want to talk to you today about the extremely important topic of...buttons! Where would we be without them? I ask you to recall how many garments you personally own that are affixed with buttons. These small, innocuous items are virtually indispensable. With what could we possible replace them? Safety pins? I think not! Masking tape? How crude! Thumb tacks? Dangerous! Buttons! Where do you suppose the original idea came from? Well, after considerable research I have discovered that the very first button was made by a Canadian Inuk, out of a whale's tooth. So that makes us—Canadians—the original button users! This is something of which to be proud...

This topic, by its insignificance, allows students to see that speaking in public does not have to be scary or threatening. It is usually easier for students to prepare silly speeches as a beginning project, then to tackle topics calling for more eloquence later.

- OTHER WAYS TO MODEL
  1. Recite memorized poetry to the class.
  2. Speak clearly for one minute about any topic suggested by the students and have students watch and listen specifically for errors in transmission, such as repetition, fidgeting, long pauses, overuse of words such as "um" et cetera. You might want to make specific errors for students to identify.

3. Begin a short speech with an interesting quotation. After you have delivered the speech to the class, ask them to identify positives and negatives about it.

I believe the many components of the language arts curriculum, the outstanding importance of mastery in this area, and teacher recognition of this importance justify the relatively high number of pages I have dedicated to Language Arts. As philosopher and sometime elementary school teacher Ludwig Wittgenstein stated, "The limits of my language mean the limits of my world." Let's strive to open up our students' worlds.

Chapter 4: Science Starters

The whole of science is nothing more than a refinement of everyday thinking.

Albert Einstein, Physics and Reality

Science is one of the few subjects that usually have built-in motivators or sets because the lessons are tangible and the materials tend to utilize all or most of the senses. In addition, teachers' manuals in Science are filled with excellent ideas for attention getting. Therefore, in this chapter I will attempt to add a few ideas that are perhaps not as obvious to the Science teacher as star charts, microscopes, magnifying glasses, beakers of fluids, bunsen burners, live insects and so on.

- ENVIRONMENTAL AWARENESS: Obtain beautiful scenery posters from travel agencies. Post one of a clean, colorful scene in front of the class and without saying a word, destroy it with black felt marker. Naturally, the students will question your motives. Some may think you have finally "lost it," but *all* will be attentive and focused! What you will have done is to draw attention to how our earth is being ravaged by pollution. Other posters or travel brochures can be passed around for discussion or reporting of how such lovely places could be protected from destruction.

- FREE FLYING: Without explanation, begin blowing up balloons and letting them go. They will, as you know, fly around wildly as the air escapes. Students will quickly focus on the escaping air, and be ready for a lesson about air.

- EINSTEIN: Enter the class in a white lab coat, wig, and glasses, and introduce yourself as Albert Einstein. Doing this will capture students' attention for a lesson on electricity or whatever you wish!

- SCIENCE MUSIC: Entering a classroom where a specific sound is heard is an instant attention getter. Have students enter the darkened room and sit quietly until you explain what is going on. The type of music playing will depend on your lesson and exactly how you wish to focus your students. For example, whale songs (many available at record stores) could introduce animal intelligence or sounds of a rocket blasting off, such as can be found on sound effects recordings, could introduce a space science lesson. There are many sound effects that make appropriate sets for science. Be sure not to overlook them.

- PHYSICAL WEIGHT CHANGES: Here is a good set for lessons on gravity. As soon as students are seated, tell them you are going to hypnotize them. (Of course, you do not actually do this.) Speaking slowly and monotonously, tell them to close their eyes and press very hard with the palms of their hands on their desks. Tell them the pressure on their hands is getting greater and greater. Their hands are stuck to the desks. Continue in this manner for a couple of minutes, then say that when you clap, their hands will suddenly unstick and float freely in the air. Because they have been applying force for an extended period, their arms will feel unnaturally light when released. Ask them how their arms and hands feel and suggest that the feeling of lightness is what they would experience in outer space where there is no gravity, or on the moon where there is little gravity. The opposite effect can be achieved by having someone apply pressure to a partner's arms as the partner holds his or her arms out. Trust me, students will be focused!

- SMOKE GETS IN YOUR EYES: Without saying a word, burn something oily but safe and play the 1950s recording by The Platters of "Smoke Gets in Your Eyes." Then introduce this Jerome Kern love song with something like, "When this song was first introduced in 1933, it referred to symbolic smoke...not real smoke. Today, with our atmosphere the way it is, it would mean something quite different." You and your students can compare the earth's atmosphere then or in the late fifties with that of today for a powerful Science lesson.

- OBJECT MEMORY: As a set for a lesson where the skill of observation is required, place about 20 small objects on the overhead projector, and cover with a cloth or piece of paper. Suitable items include paper clips, thumb tacks, push pins, safety pins, small nail scissors, a needle, an elastic band, a ring, a compass and any science lab equipment that is small enough to fit in with the other items. Give each student a piece of paper, then tell students to number to 20 and get ready for a game. Remove the cloth for 30 seconds, then recover the items. Students must remember the items they observed.

- WATCH CLOSELY NOW: This set is also preparation for a lesson on observation skills and the importance of really looking. Tell the students to look at you. Stand there in front of them for about 30 seconds, then leave the room, make a few subtle changes in your appearance, and return. Depending on your sex, you can make such pre-planned changes as these: removal of one earring, a single button opened or closed, one sock pushed down, a change in your facial expression, an elastic band around your wrist or finger. See how quickly students can discover the changes. Often, they note details that are not changes at all. This can lead to excellent discussions about how we observe and record observations in Science.

- AIR POLLUTION: Begin the class by saying you have a joke to share, but you are wondering if students will be able to "get it." (This challenge always encourages more concentrated listening—if just to prove to you that students *can* get the joke which is, as follows:

  According to scientists, inhaling the air of any big city is like smoking two packs of cigarettes a day! I can just see the ads of the future! I breathe Toronto—it satisfies!

A lesson on air pollution, density, or composition could follow.

- CHANGE: Set for a lesson on change, of which science is the study, with a joke such as the following:

  You go to a museum and see hairy, grizzled men cooking meat outside their shelters. Then thousands of years of evolution and progress pass. Nonetheless, what do you see on a Sunday afternoon?—hairy, grizzled men cooking meat outside their shelters.

Discuss and enjoy. Lead the discussion to the idea of change (metamorphosis) in whatever Science topic you are studying. Keep your eyes open for other science-oriented jokes, too, and begin your own file.

• SOLAR SYSTEM: To begin a unit on the solar system, one of my colleagues once used the following effective set. On her classroom door, she put a big, bright sign:

> NEW SHOW PREVIEWING TODAY
> CAST OF THOUSANDS
> EVERYONE OF THEM A STAR...

The students entered the class, already set, interested and eager to see what the poster was all about!

• SCIENTIFIC QUOTATIONS: Although difficult to come by, quotations specific to the study of science can be found and used effectively as sets. Teachers would be wise to collect these special quotations as they come across them and to save them in special files. In addition to the quotation at the beginning of this chapter, the following are good examples:

> True science teaches, above all, to doubt and be ignorant.
>
> *Miguel De Unamuno*

> Man has wrested from nature the power to make the world a desert or to make the deserts bloom. There is no evil in the atom; only men's souls.
>
> *Adlai Stevenson* (1952)

As I mentioned at the beginning of this chapter, Science lends itself to sets using attention-getting items. A particularly good source of items is a public science centre. Such a centre often has a bookstore not only with wonderful books, including science game books, but many other items and ideas appropriate for science sets too. For example, I have found such inexpensive items as spinning tops (gravity, centrifugal force...), slides of unusual insects (biology) and three-dimensional illustrations of the solar system on everything from key chains to jewellery. A visit to a science centre can be well worth your time.

Chapter 5: Motivators for Mathematics

> Mathematics...possesses not only truth, but supreme beauty.
>
> *Bertrand Russell, The Study of Mathematics*

Math consists largely of individual work, correcting, and more individual work, and its content makes creativity difficult. Just as Gertrude Stein said, "Rose is a rose is a rose...," I say, "Math is math is math...." Nevertheless, preparing interesting sets, difficult though it may be, is not impossible. We are what we repeatedly do. Excellence in teaching, then, no matter what the subject, is not just an act, but a habit. It is up to the teacher to make it a habit to teach with pizzazz, to accept the challenge of teaching math with an enthusiasm that will help to draw the students in.

I am reminded of one of my math teachers who made math (usually a horror for me) a joy! When I think back, it was not the content of the course he made interesting, but the way in which he delivered it that drew me in. He was witty, spontaneous, and unpredictable. Once he attempted a clumsy cartwheel in front of the class to illustrate a 360° turn. Another time he was unsuccessfully trying to whirl a hula hoop around his waist as we entered the room. Awestruck, we all sat silently and watched until he stopped his frantic wiggling and solemnly declared, "Yes...this is a circle... not to be confused with a sphere." He then produced a beach ball from behind his desk and bounced it off one of the boy's heads. I realize now what a truly wonderful set that was.

But sometimes, his sets were less obvious. For example, he always met us at the door, sparkling with excitement and such comments as, "Welcome to the world of rational numbers, Miss Jones," and "Today we will explore the thrilling concept of algebra in action, Mr. Blair, so hurry to your seat—don't miss a single moment!" In these instances, I now realize that he, himself, was the set for his lessons. He was Merlin the Magician, Houdini, Santa Claus, Malcolm X...or anyone else he chose to be. Math was still math, but the students could hardly wait to go to his classes, whether they loved or hated the subject. His attitude, his very presence, made us want to learn, and we did.

Once when I met that math teacher in a supermarket, I was hard pressed to recognize him, a nondescript little man pushing a grocery cart. Then I realized that teachers really are actors, their classrooms are their stages, and their students, their captive audiences. I learned much more than math from that one teacher. Now, when my load seems heavy and I know I am not properly setting my classes, I recall him and summon up all the extra adrenalin I can to teach. You can do this too! Nothing great was ever achieved without enthusiasm.

Math may be one of those subjects where the focus comes largely from reminding students what they are working on and telling them what page to turn to, but the teacher's attitude contributes significantly to students' motivation. And there are instances, particularly at the outset of a new unit, when a snappy set does wonders. Consider the following, but do not overlook the sets suggested in teachers' manuals. Those sets have been created by persons much more knowledgeable in the field than I.

- PEANUT SCRAMBLE: Yes, this is exactly what it sounds like. Give each student a paper cup, scatter peanuts around your room, and let them "go for it." With younger students (Grades 1-3), the peanuts can then be used for one-to-one correspondence or simple problems and operations, for example. With older students, have groups of about three, and ask members to create fractions from their three different numbers of peanuts or problems using mathematical operations, for example, what percentage of all the peanuts do I have? The peanuts are simply a tool and an attention getter to begin the class. They can be used in any way you see fit. I usually allow the students to shell and eat the peanuts only after all assigned work has been completed; hence, there is built-in positive reinforcement, too!

- JOKES: Beginning a math class with an appropriate joke on the overhead can set the scene for more serious work. In addition, it shows the students that math can be fun. (For some, this is hard to believe!) Locating appropriate math jokes is difficult, so I suggest that, if you do teach math, you keep your eyes open and begin your own file. Since I do not teach this subject, my "math chuckles" are limited, but perhaps I can get you started.

    (use name of student in class): How many fish have you caught so far?
    (another student): Well, if I catch this one I'm after right now, then catch two more, I'll have three!

This joke could lead Grade 2 students into a lesson on addition. See Appendix C for a few more ideas.

- MATH GAMES: Some books deal specifically with math games. Purchasing one of these from a bookstore, convention, or catalogue that comes to the school librarian can be very worthwhile. One example is *Games for Math* by Peggy Kage (Pantheon Books), recommended for Grades 1-4.

- BALL DROP: For a Junior High class, locate as many different-sized balls as possible: from a tiny, marble-sized high bouncer to a large beach ball. Say you will play a guessing game. First, measure the circumference of one of the medium-sized balls then figure out the diameter. Now have students (in pairs if you wish) guess these dimensions for all the other balls. Then you can ask, "Which ball will hit the floor first...bounce the highest...roll the furthest...," to get them thinking about speed, size, mass, distance and so on.

- BODIES TO SCALE: On an overhead or chart-paper, show a badly proportioned drawing of a person's silhouette. Tell the students this is a self-portrait. No doubt there will be laughter and perhaps some not-so-nice comments, but laugh along with them and then ask what is wrong. Try to extract the idea of "scale drawings" from them (even if they do not actually use that term). Then demonstrate how to make a scale drawing using string and their rulers. For example, measure an arm with string, then measure the string against a ruler to find out the length of the arm. Have them work in pairs to draw silhouettes of themselves. In addition to being a good set for scale drawing, this activity can be used for measurement and measurement conversions.

- MATH MUNCHIES: Ask students to close their eyes and place one hand, palm up, on their desks. Then explain that what you are putting in their hands are math munchies, which will give them extra strength to handle that day's class. I once used M&M's with a Grade 4 class about to be introduced to long division, one of a math teacher's all-time horrors, but *anything* would have worked. The "magic" is the game (close your eyes, etc.) and in your telling the students that you empathize with them. Some dear students assured me that the M&M's "really did help us learn..."

- MATH EXCUSES: Every teacher knows that students can sit looking directly at you, seemingly attentive, but be somewhere else entirely. Try beginning a particularly hard math class with excuses on the overhead or chalkboard. The focus, while not specifically on a math concept, is more on the concentration necessary to learn a difficult skill.

QUESTION: **Why do you always daydream in math?"**

- Because I forgot to do it during Social Studies!
- Is this math class? I thought it was Language Arts.
- I wasn't daydreaming. I was having an out-of-body experience.
- I'm doing geometry. I'm thinking about the Bermuda Triangle.
- I'm doing math. I'm figuring out how many days until my birthday.

Allow students a few moments to discuss and ponder the question, then review with them the suggested reasons and ask for a few of their own. Be sure to conclude in such a way that you give the rationale for what you have just done. "We all agree that paying attention in math is really hard, but today's lesson is so important that I want you each to make an extra effort...." You can also generate questions and excuses about why it is so hard to remember math formulas, learn math time tables, do homework, and the like. The important thing is to empathize with your math students and provide encouragement for the day's lesson.

- EDIBLES: Food is always a great motivator, but in a subject as objective as Mathematics, we tend to forget this. Here is a great set for a lesson on division, rational numbers, measurement, or even geometry. Simply bring a large, rectangular pan of Rice Krispies squares to class (it doesn't *have* to be Rice Krispies squares, but since that's all I can make...). Tell the students the pan is for them, *after* they figure out how to divide it equally among them. And they must use their problem-solving skills to come up with more than one suggestion. Naturally, they are allowed to eat the set afterwards.

- SUGAR CUBE CONSTRUCTIONS: Pass out baggies with about 20-25 sugar cubes per baggie to students or student pairs and ask them to build something in 10 minutes or less. They will be curious, but do not say anything else at this time. This activity is a set for a lesson on measurement, volume, and capacity. After students have finished building, you can have them count all the showing faces, measure the height and width, find the surface area, estimate the mass and volume, and make scale drawings of their creations.

- FORCED OUT: The goal of this set game is *not* to be the player forced to say "100." Decide who will start. The first player names any number from 1 to 10. The next player adds a number (1-10) and gives the answer. The third player adds a number to this total, and so on. The highest number a player can say without penalty is 99. The next player must say "plus one equals 100" and is, therefore, out. Then you begin a new round. Any operation can be substituted for the addition. This highly motivating set prepares for work on basic operations and gives practice at the same time.

  Note: People are not out if they make errors in their answers. Simply correct and continue.

Finding or creating interesting and motivating sets for math is difficult, but possible. When I am teaching Math, and struggling with this part of my lesson plans, I continually remind myself of this maxim: In the presence of trouble, some people buy crutches; others grow wings. I am still working on my wings; in the meantime, I use crutches once in a while!

Chapter 6:   Sets for the Social Sciences

Man is a social animal.

Benedict Spinoza, Ethics

The teaching of any of the social sciences, including health, sociology, courses concerned with peer relationships, and social studies, creates particular challenges for the teacher. These subjects revolve around people, so much of the material is sensitive in nature. Obviously delicate topics are sex education and suicide; however, even eighteenth and nineteenth century Canadian history can require careful handling in light of the increasingly multicultural face of our country, the flow of new immigrants and concern over portrayals of native peoples.

Students, as a rule, enjoy these studies that can be so pertinent to their lives, but still require focusing before the lesson begins. The value of stimulating sets, where, for example, you can make history "come alive" cannot be overestimated. Shakespeare said, "All the world's a stage, and all the men and women merely players." I agree, and the theatrics of teaching can really be emphasized in teaching the social sciences. Human drama, human history, and human society as it has developed over time are truly exciting. Make them even more exciting with dramatically presented sets.

This curriculum area above all others seems to have inspired the development of kits with wonderful sets. Do not overlook them in your eagerness to get on to the meat of a lesson. Several of the sets that I have provided require longer than the recommended five minutes, but their impact can be spread over several lessons or even complete units of study. Once a set has been established, you can reset by reminding students of the initial set. Remember that the success of all sets is determined by the initial impact the set has on students.

- HAVES AND HAVE-NOTS: Pass around a container with one slip of paper for each student. Eighty percent of the slips will be one color; the other 20 percent, a different color. Offer no explanations. Then tell students they will be given an easy quiz, and all those who get 100 percent will receive a reward of some kind (see pages 16-17). Tell them they must clear their desks and use only those materials provided by you. Then give paper and pencils to the 80 percent, but paper only to the 20 percent. Give a simple oral test asking such questions as, "What is the opposite of night?" and "What is the name of our school?" The 20 percent group will complain and ask for pencils; ignore their protests. Mark the "test" together quickly and distribute prizes to the 80 percent group. I am sure you can see where we are going with this: the 20 percent represent the developing nations of the world. This activity will really get the students thinking!

  You can use the same strategy to explore purchasing power, with the wealthy (20%), the impoverished (40%) and the middle class (40%) represented. I have used Monopoly money here, but you can make pretend money using a photocopier. Money is distributed to everyone according to their class. Then you "sell" basic items (identified on slips of paper) such as food, homes, and clothing, for which the "poor" will not have enough money. Again, this activity leads to heated discussions and much thought about social systems. Even very young children can relate to a simplified version of this set. The important point to be made is that students had no choice in deciding to which group they would belong — neither do the disadvantaged! Because the students will have had direct experience in being haves or have-nots, you can simply refer back to it and their accompanying feelings for future lesson focuses.

- DRESS-UP: Whatever unit of study you are covering in Social Studies, there are specific items of apparel that you could wear to class to create an instant set. For example, for a unit on pioneers, you could wear a long dress, apron, and hat or frock coat and old hat. (Check costume books or the nearest pioneer village to see what costume pieces would best evoke pioneer times in your community.) You can find costume pieces at local costume stores and rental agencies, through letters to parents (it's amazing what they can come up with), by asking the other staff, and by checking out senior citizens' homes (where some residents may have interesting clothing stored away).

- APPROPRIATE QUOTATIONS: Beginning any lesson with a quotation both visible (overhead) and auditory (read aloud) is an instant set. Plan to collect a few quotations and even jokes appropriate for teaching in the Social Sciences. You can also create your own as I sometimes do. Here are a few ideas.

  - "Personally, I'm against sex ed. If you look at the statistics, what you guys need is a course on "How Not To." (This is appropriate for Junior High Sex Education classes; it helps to relax the atmosphere.)
  - "The computer is one of the great inventions of our time. There are still as many mistakes as ever, but now they are "nobody's fault." (This fun focus is suitable for any Junior High Social Studies lesson about our changing world and its effects on people.)

- GIBBERISH: Ask students to pair up as quickly as possible and decide who is A and who, B. A must ask how to get to the nearest washroom, and B must give the directions. However, both students must talk in gibberish only. Allow the pairs to try this for a few moments, then have the class discuss how difficult communication was. Relate the issue to a lesson pertaining to the problems caused by language barriers.

- ALIEN: Write "ALIEN" on the board in large, colored letters. When all students have noticed it, ask who thinks they know what an alien is. There will be many raised hands and just as many wild and wonderful descriptions of monsters and creatures from outer space. Accept these, but then suggest that the students themselves could be aliens. Their first reaction will probably be "oh sure...on another planet." Your goal is to lead them to the realization that any person who is totally out of his or her usual environment is an alien. For example, if one of them parachuted into a remote African village, he or she would probably be seen as an alien. You can then lead students into a discussion of new immigrants in Canada, how they feel, why they behave the way they do and so on. This quick set can lead in many directions.

- A CHARACTER FROM THE PAST: This set is one of my favorites, and if you ever saw the movie *Teachers* with Nick Nolte, you will recognize it. Dress up as a famous character from history, step into the role of actor, and begin the class with an oration or statement by that person: for instance, Abraham Lincoln reciting "Fourscore and seven years ago..." or Winston Churchill, "Never in the field of human conflict was so much owed by so many to so few." Doing so makes a stimulating set for a history lesson about the particular time period of the person. Look to the drama department of your own school or a neighboring one for evocative costume bits. Or turn to local colleges, universities, theatre groups or even a costume rental outlet. As a last resort, if you are unable to locate a costume, you can attach a large sign to your chest to indicate who you are and assume the character of that person at the beginning of the class.

- A LOOK AT THE PAST: This set involves the use of old magazines, papers or catalogues from the past, none of which are as difficult to locate as you might suppose. I went to a senior citizens' home once and came away with a treasure trove in borrowed photographs, seed catalogues, and old textbooks. Grandparents often have such items stored away in attics or cedar chests, and are happy to share them with you. Once located, any of these materials make wonderful, exciting sets for history lessons and provide much information relevant to their eras. For example, I found a 1941 Home Economics Teacher's Manual and was amused and delighted by its contents, which readily illustrated how values change over time. One section, entitled "Preparing for Your Man to Arrive Home," included such suggestions as these: meet him at the door with a soothing drink, his slippers and the newspaper; be sure the house is clean and dinner is ready; be sure you are not wearing an apron and that you look your best; under no circumstances allow the children to annoy him as he has worked hard and is very tired. In addition to giving my class a good laugh, this piece gave us insights into past values.

- POLITICAL CARTOONS: Many of the political cartoons carried in daily newspapers are suitable for putting on an overhead and using as a set for a lesson on current events, government, or local affairs. Doing so provides a fast, easy set, not to be overlooked.

- MUSIC THAT TAKES US BACK: Set the history lesson by playing a piece of music specific to that period. For example, black soul music could lead nicely into discussions of slavery and songs such as "Dixie," the American Civil War. Handel's "Hallelujah Chorus," or even the playing of "God Save The Queen," could provide a set for lessons on the British monarchy. Much "time period" music is available from local libraries or even from seniors in the neighborhood.

- STORYTELLERS: I have discovered that elderly people in the neighborhood simply love to be guests at school and to share personal stories of the past. One old gentleman kept my Grade 7 class entranced for nearly an hour with tales of his survival in a log cabin in sub-zero temperatures. My set (I had expected him to speak for no more than 10 minutes) became my entire lesson, but it was one the students never forgot. If the elderly people you know are unwilling to come to your class, they will probably at least share photos and other artifacts with you.

- PHOTO DISPLAY: A display of photos of the early years of your city, for example, makes a wonderful set for studying the city's history. Check the local museums, historical societies, archives or even newspapers for photos you can borrow to create a live look into the past.

- OVERHEAD MAP: Have the lights off and put a simple map you have made on the overhead. The map can either be of your classroom or of the entire school. Let the students work with partners to locate a hidden "treasure" by following simple written or oral map-reading clues. For example, clues might include (a) begin at the NW corner; (b) move 3 m S and 1 m E....When students think they have determined the treasure site, have them check with you. The first pair to locate the treasure wins, but all get rewards. Naturally, students must work out clues in their heads, not by getting up and moving around. The idea is to interest them in map reading for a Geography lesson.

- PASS-IT-ON: This is a simple, quick set for a class in Social Studies or Health, particularly on the topics of relating to friends and getting along with others. Move to the student closest to you, give that student a big smile and say, "Pass it on." Students quickly realize that not smiling at someone who is smiling at you is almost impossible. You can take the exercise a step further by having one student *try* not to smile, while others smile at him.

- GOOD WORD: For a lesson dealing with the communication of feelings between individuals and even countries, try this set. Pass a container with folded slips of paper on which there are numbers, words, symbols, whatever, as long as there are pairs. Every student will thereby end up with a partner by chance. Allow a few seconds for students to move close to their partners, then tell them that their job is to say at least two sincere, positive statements to each other. Doing this can be difficult, especially if the partners do not know each other well, so begin by giving them a simple discussion topic. Let them talk to each other for about two minutes, then allow them about 60 seconds to consider each other closely and come up with the two positive statements. The extra benefits from this set are that everyone feels good after it is over, and you have a happy group with which to work!

- NAMES: Find at least one book on "what to name your baby," then locate the name of each student in your class, and mark the page. Now, if you have many students with unusual names, you can either find names as close as possible to theirs or ask their parents for the necessary information. To set your lesson, say specifically to one student (I usually choose one who is frequently more difficult to focus), "Did you know that your name means _____, and that it comes from the Latin word _____?" You will have the students' undivided attention, particularly if the name description does not fit the particular student. Go on with either all the name meanings, or just a few (in which case you *must* give more name meanings in subsequent classes until all the students have heard their names). The value of this set is that it leads nicely into lessons on such different topics as nationalities, name fads, family roots, self-esteem and family structure. This "name game," as I have come to call it, can be stretched to fit many lessons, and the students like nothing better than hearing about themselves.

Note: If you simply cannot come up with a meaning for a name, ask the students to help you to *create* one. Doing this can be a lot of fun too!

- THE DREAM: Begin the lesson by telling students that you have had the most unusual dream about them! Tell them that you dreamed they were all in their thirties and were well established in their careers. Then, student by student, tell each one what you "saw" him or her doing in your dream. You will have to spend a bit of time preparing for this, but if you know your students (and what teacher doesn't?) preparation will be easy. What you are setting is a lesson on careers, responsibility, or growing up. The key is to choose occupations for students that are totally inappropriate. For example, say that the shy girl will become prime minister of Canada and the "jock," a star ballet dancer. In this way, feelings will not be hurt and the students will appreciate the humor of visualizing themselves in your chosen roles.

- POPULATION EXPLOSION: As part of a set for Social Studies or Sex Education, tell the students they are going to participate in a game that will reveal something to them about life. Their goal is to try to guess what that insight is. Bring several small area rugs, such as bathroom rugs, or similarly sized pieces of cardboard. Place about three on the floor (depending on class size) and encourage as many students as possible to crowd onto one mat. If everyone stands on one foot and holds onto other players, as many as 20 people should fit on one rug. Encourage co-operation, not competition. Then discuss the situation:
  - What did it feel like?
  - Did anyone suffer from claustrophobia?
  - Do we ever have to be in situations like this?
  - Consider the word "population," and try to figure out why we did this.

  Students should realize that we are lucky not to be faced with the overpopulation problems of other countries.

Lessons in such subjects as Health and History usually offer many different possibilities for sets. Whether or not you can use any of my specific suggestions, I hope I have been able to inspire you to create and use some of your own.

Chapter 7:   All-occasion Eye-Openers

Look for opportunities, *not* guarantees!

K. Paterson

The sets suggested here can be used in so many different ways that I have called them "all-occasion" eye-openers, or sets, and have given them their own chapter. I am quite sure that you will be able to find many more uses for them than the ones I have suggested. Remember: Getting the students' attention and focusing it on your particular topic is what you are trying to do.

- SPARKLERS: In a darkened room, light several sparklers with no other comment than "watch." I guarantee you will have instant attention. Then take it from there:
  - What makes them sparkle? (Science)
  - How did they make you feel? (Health)
  - How long did they sparkle? (Math)
  - What do they remind you of? (Language Arts (LA) writing project)

- THE PACKAGE: Bring a wrapped box of any size to class. Let students try to guess what it contains. The contents will depend upon your lesson. For example, you could capture their attention with rocks for Science, photographs for any subject or geometric shapes for Math.

- THE UNFAIR TEST: Tell students they are going to be given a surprise test (something you would *never* really do!) and that all those who get 100 percent will be given a reward (see Chapter 1, pages 16-17, for ideas). Have students list numbers 1-5 on their papers and ask them to identify each object you show them through a word or phrase. Then, solemnly hold up five items, for example, an apple, a piece of blank paper, a glass of water (drink some to show that the contents are not poisonous), a feather, and a candle. The students will correctly identify these familiar objects, but when they exchange papers for marking and you ask what answers are down, keep saying "no," "incorrect" or "wrong." The students will be getting upset. Then give the correct answers: the seed of an apple tree, the end result of a pulp and paper mill, home for a fish, a writing tool in the 1800s, a source of heat. The students will realize they have been conned, but seem serious when you ask how many got 100 percent. You can then lead into a lively discussion using the focus you have chosen.

For example:
- different points of view (LA);
- issue of not being given enough information to make an accurate observation (Science);
- examination of different ways to solve a problem; not limiting ourselves to a way when it is not working (Math);
- creation of anger, frustration, and sense of being cheated (Social Studies; LA, story writing).

- HANG-MAN: This simple childhood game still works with today's highly technical students. Make a line for each letter of the word of your choice (a word that will set the students and focus them on your lesson for the day), and allow students to guess the letters. For each incorrect guess, the letter is written beside the gallows, and another part of the victim is added. Just in case you have forgotten how the game works, here is an example with the word "geometry."

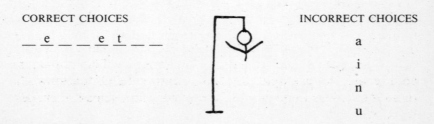

CORRECT CHOICES

_ e _ _ e t _ _

INCORRECT CHOICES

a

i

n

u

The person who guesses the word before the entire body is hanged should receive some sort of recognition (see Chapter 1, pages 16-17). Even Grade 9 students love playing this game.

- CARTOON STRIPS: Show a relevant cartoon strip on the overhead, after first turning off the lights to get student attention. Remember that the less said during a set the better, so give students a few minutes to appreciate the humor, then point out exactly how the cartoon strip relates to your lesson. I like the newspaper cartoon strips, especially late in the summer when cartoonists make the most of students preparing to return to school. In addition, the Luann books of Greg Evans, such as *Luann: School and Other Problems* (Tom Doherty Associates), have terrific strips. Other cartoon strips including *Calvin and Hobbes, Broom Hilda, Peanuts* and *Hi and Lois* might be better for providing some insight into a subject. For example, in one *Peanuts* cartoon strip, Lucy convinces Snoopy, the author, to change the word "suddenly" to "gradually" in his story, with humorous results.

Note: Be sure to include the source on the overhead and do not violate copyright laws.

- PENCIL PUZZLES: These include mazes and connecting-the-dots activities which you can alter to suit. The way in which you make them work as sets is that the puzzle must relate to the lesson, for example, a maze through a swamp (Science) or a maze through a pyramid (Social Studies). More elaborate paper and pencil game books are available in childrens' bookstores, too. Steve Ryan's *Pencil Puzzlers*, published by Sterling, is one of my particular favorites.

- BALLOON BURSTS: A fun set, which requires a bit of preparation, is balloon bursting. In blown-up balloons, kept for convenience in large garbage bags, store small slips of paper. What is *on* the papers depends upon your lesson: math problems, essay topics, science questions, whatever. Each student chooses a balloon and has two minutes to break it creatively. (Have a pin on hand for those few who just cannot seem to break theirs!) Then individuals follow whatever directions are inside their balloons. Once Junior High students of mine discovered questions on AIDS in their balloons. They were given half the class to answer those questions by themselves, then half to share their answers. The balloons made this otherwise routine assignment magical.

- THE MASK: For an effective set, don a plain, white, neutral mask, such as can be obtained from theatrical, costume and magic stores, while outside the room or with your back turned. Now drape a scarf or towel over your head. The effect is startling, but it is how you use it that becomes the set. For example:
  - Write on the board: *I cannot talk, but I have feelings just like you. See how many of them you can identify.* Then, using extreme body language, demonstrate emotions such as nervousness, shyness, and anger. The set works for lessons on body language (Health), non-verbal communication (LA), emotions (Social Studies; Health) and others.
  - The wearing of the neutral mask can also point out that despite the playing of a variety of roles the same person is underneath. A student teacher once enacted some of her roles with Grade 7 students, spurring them to write thoughtful pieces about roles and the personalities associated with them.

- VISUAL IMAGERY: Ask the students if they have ever heard about patients who have miraculously cured themselves through visual imagery. (Finding an article or two about this is helpful, but unnecessary.) Be serious, and tell them you are going to help them to tap into the imaging abilities that they all have, so that learning will be easier. Use the following steps:

1. Sit comfortably and close your eyes.
2. Breathe deeply and slowly. Count your breaths.
3. Concentrate on your brain...visualize what you think it looks like...feel its weight...texture. Focus all thoughts on your head and brain.
4. Imagine that tiny part of your brain that is responsible for learning and look closely at it. Concentrate on it for 30 seconds...keep bringing your thoughts back to it.
5. Now, in that special area, you can see an army of tiny white knights fighting to make you learn, to let you remember... Look at them! They are your power—your strength. You can control them if you can visualize them clearly.
6. There are also black knights there who are fighting the white knights...they are trying to prevent you from learning...but they are weak...you can control them too. They are dying. The white knights are winning....

Note: Even if only a few are able to master this technique and can generalize it to other situations, you have been successful!

Alumni students have returned to visit me and told me how they still use visual imagery.

- THE BOX REVISITED: Do not forget all the wonderful and magical items you have collected in The Box (see Chapter 2, pages 23-24). Whenever you lack a prepared set and are faced with a restless, unfocused group, delve into The Box. Doing this requires quick creativity and imagination—something *all* teachers have whether they realize it or not! Take a fast scan of the contents and you may find something that you can adapt to fit the upcoming lesson. Based on the contents of my Box, here are a few examples of instant sets that I have done.

  1. With a large feather as a quill, I asked, "Can you imagine what it would be like to have to write our stories with this?" The set introduced the reading of a story set in the 1800s.
  2. Using a small, beanbag clown doll, I asked, "What is this?" (A thing.) Then I tossed and caught it. "What am I doing with it?" (An action.) The lesson focused on nouns and verbs.

- CANDID CAMERA: To prepare for this set, you must take a candid photo of each student in the class. Doing this is not as difficult as it seems: most students love to get their pictures taken. At a later date, these photos, mounted on construction paper for easy handling, are passed out to the students as soon as they enter the class. Instant attention! However, before handing out the photos, tell students that they must remain in their seats until after directions are given, at which time you will allow two minutes for photo sharing; anyone who breaks this rule will lose his or her photo. Individual photos can be used as sets in numerous ways, including the following:

  1. Give students the photos of themselves and assign the writing of an autobiography which will begin with a current-day description. Give photos out randomly and ask each student to do a character analysis of the person in his/her photo. (LA)
  2. Pass photos out randomly and ask each student to provide several opinions, factual observations, and a hypothesis about the person in focus. (Science)
  3. Use the photos for numerous art class sets such as portrait sketching and cartooning. In this case, the set may become the lesson itself. Not every set needs to be separate from the lesson it precedes. (Art)

- POETRY AND LIMERICKS: The use of poetry and limericks in snappy sets can be easily overlooked, partly because many students do not like poetry. However, if you choose a poem that has something to do with your lesson, you can draw the discussion in that direction. For example, use Dennis Lee's "William Lyon Mackenzie King" to introduce a study of that Canadian prime minister. Have the poem on the overhead, cue for attention, then either read in unison or read the poem aloud yourself. Be sure to choose a poem that is easy to interpret, a ballad being an example. If the poem is long, select only a relevant portion. And do not forget to consider poems written for children.

- THE GLASS CONTAINER: With so many beautiful, clear glass containers available, simply choose one and stick with it. I personally like the tall, slim cylinders which are, I believe, intended as bud vases. I have three such containers of differing heights. Usually, they are filled with pretty colored marbles, but when I need an instant set, they become magical vessels of interest. They can hold anything you want them to, depending, of course, on your lesson. Also, the students will notice them as soon as they enter your class. The vases might hold colored water, water and oil, seeds, or different kinds of soil, all for Science; real flowers for story and letter writing in Language Arts; pasta pieces for Art, Health and Social Studies; and rice for a Social Studies topic on what countries rely on that food. As you can see, you are limited only by your own imagination. Once, in a desperate attempt to help my students think creatively before undertaking a task...*any* task...I filled my glass container with real nuts and bolts and proudly set it on my desk. After a few seconds of puzzled looks, students began questioning this act. "You decide," I told them, "why I might have done this. Think of as many reasons as possible, no matter how ridiculous they may seem." I was amazed at the wonderful answers they came up with including these:

  - to test the strength of the glass;
  - to make a pop-art decoration;
  - to illustrate opposites (glass/metal);
  - and...to drive us crazy trying to think of reasons why our teacher would fill a beautiful jar with dirty old junk!

So, as soon as the students see your container, your set is established! You have their attention, and now you can teach!

- THE CRYSTAL: Many stores sell beautiful glass crystals for hanging in windows to catch the light. I use my crystal to catch students' attention, as well. Simply hold the crystal up in front of the class and peer mysteriously into it. No words are necessary. Try shining a light through it, holding it near direct sun, or placing it on the overhead projector with the lights off. "Great," you say, "but how does this create a set?" That is up to you, but here are a few ways in which you could use it:

  - to study light, refraction, elements and the sun (Science);
  - to ask how many "faces" the crystal has and have students create mathematical problems involving operations based on this fact (Math);
  - to stimulate story writing (what if it were a magic crystal or worth a million dollars and the student lost it?) (LA).

- GENTLE PERSUASION: Sound effects always create great sets, but this particular series, *Gentle Persuasion*, (The Special Music Company and Pair Records Division of Essex Entertainment Inc., 560 Sylvan Ave., Englewood Cliffs, N.J. 07632) has proven especially useful to me, particularly at the upper elementary and Junior High levels. Ask students to sit comfortably, turn off the lights, and play a portion of the tape of your choice. The effect is almost magical; the sounds on the tape tend to lull students into a sort of meditational state. Using my favorite tape, "Sounds of the Tropical Rain Forest," as an example, you can then invite students to write descriptions of the places they imagined, explore the issue of the destruction of our tropical rain forests, count how many different birds they heard, or consider in what climate, country or continent the sounds might have been set.

- JUST FOR THE FUN OF IT: As soon as you want to begin the class, stand and begin making ridiculous commands. Assume that the students will obey them. For example, you could say, "Put a finger on your nose....Stick out your tongue...." Students are always eager to do something different and you will probably find that all are soon following the directions. Then pause, look at them and say something like, "Boy, you guys look funny!" They will realize that they have been tricked and laughter will erupt. Ask them to sit down, then lead the activity into your lesson which might be on the Social Studies issue of conformity, following rules, leaders/followers, or respect; writing or reading about something equally silly; or exploring how people's tendency to follow a crowd might help the save-the-environment campaign.

- BUSINESS CARDS: Have you ever noticed how many creative, bizarre business cards are in use? My favorite is a hot pink card that says "FOUR PAWS ONLY" and gives a phone number for a dog grooming parlour. Collecting many cards in a short time can be easily done by asking peers to empty pockets and purses and give you cards they have no use for. Then these can create an amusing set for almost any subject area. For instance, you can hand them out (I always allow time for trading) and invite students to do any of the following:

  - to become the owners of their cards and introduce themselves; to write biographies about the persons featured; to write dialogues between themselves and the card owners... (LA);
  - to create some word problems that are in some way related to the cards they have; to count the number of words and the number of letters on their cards, create some ratios between the two, and explain how they did this (Math).

- MOVIE/VIDEO POSTERS: Video stores will give away outdated movie posters—you just have to be there at the right time. Posters, whether they are of movies the students have seen or not, make wonderful, colorful sets. For example, the poster from *Whispers in the Dark* makes an excellent story starter for Language Arts; the poster for *Aladdin* is great for writing dialogue. Many film posters are instant sets for issues in Social Studies, Health, and Science. And the best part is—they are free!

- NOVELTY STORES: I cannot overemphasize the importance of locating and visiting novelty stores in your area. Even if you do not buy anything, you will find wonderful items that cannot fail to give you ideas. These stores are filled with stamps, stickers, games, novelties, posters, puzzles and so on. I defy any teacher to enter one without coming away with at least one new idea. In one I purchased a toy microphone for only $2. Now just think of all the ways in which you could use one in your class!

The sets suggested in this chapter can be used in almost any subject area with just a little imagination and leading discussion. Even if your set catches everyone's attention, focuses students on you, but falls short of turning the students on to your topic, at least you will have gained their attention to tell them exactly what you still plan to do. And that's a good start! Encourage yourself to use eye-openers to introduce your lessons, and soon they will no longer seem like wastes of time, but as enjoyable activities.

Chapter 8: Refocusing Attention

If at first you don't succeed—it's hard to hide
your astonishment!

K. Paterson

The Problem

Something was terribly wrong! My students were not working hard
independently; instead, a hive of escalating off-task activities had
come into being. Whispering was intensifying, as was pencil
sharpening, book dropping, paper rustling, giggling and socializ-
ing. Where had I gone wrong? My anticipatory set had been excellent, leaving all the students motivated to begin writing their opinions
of modern music. We had brainstormed for ways to get started,
and indeed, until a few minutes ago, they *had* all started. Now, it
appeared, they had all stopped! And we still had 15 minutes of writing time left! "Don't panic!" a little voice cried out to me,
"*Refocus!*"

The Solution

Refocusing is different from initial focusing or motivating through
an anticipatory set. Instead of beginning a lesson, it takes place
somewhere in the middle when students seem to have lost their focus.
Unlike anticipatory sets, refocusing activities such as those suggested
in this chapter do not necessarily relate to the task at hand. The
purpose of a refocuser is to grab all the students' wandering atten-

tions and turn them on you so that you can refocus attention correctly. If you do not break the cycle of inappropriate behaviors that have begun, the behaviors will continue to escalate.

Since the students know they are supposed to be working, you cannot just have them play a game without an explanation. This is what works for me: "Hey guys!" (I like this casual, unisex term.) "We seem to be getting off target here. There is too much talking and not enough working. Let's take a time out, then get back at it with some real effort." Naturally, the exact words are unimportant, but this is the general message you wish to get across!

Refocusers are time outs. They bring the class back together in a common activity, but then you must return attention to the original task. Without this last action, the refocuser becomes just another off-task behavior. As a result, as soon as you have used a refocuser, act upon these three Rs:

The Three Rs

1. **REMIND:** Review quickly what exactly the students were doing before the time out.
   Example: "Now that we are all together again, let's get back to writing those opinion essays. Remember that you were to...."

2. **REASSURE:** Let students know that getting stuck and requiring assistance at this time is OK.
   Example: "I realize that getting started is the hardest thing, so if you are having problems, raise your hand and I'll come to you."

3. **REINFORCE:** Let them know once again what your specific expectations are.
   Example: "We have 15 minutes left to work on these essays. By then I'll expect to see at least your outlines and rough drafts. We will continue to work on these essays tomorrow and you will hand in the finished copies after that class for marking."

Refocusing activities can be used over and over again with equal impact. You probably have many of your own already, but maybe some of the following will be new to you:

- KEEP THE RHYTHM: Have students sit straight in their desks, hands relaxed on desktops. Begin a clapping or desk tapping rhythm. Point to someone, who adds to the sequence. When all have the two-part pattern, point to another and so on. After a few minutes of this, everyone will have had a break, and you can institute the three Rs.

- SILENT LISTENING: Tell (don't ask) all students to put their heads on their desks, to close their eyes, and to listen to a piece of classical music selected by you. They may complain, especially the older ones, so give them the choice of doing this or an extra work sheet. (Soon all heads will be down.) Choose music that is calming, for example, *Sleeping Beauty* by Tchaikovsky, lullabies by Brahms, waltzes by Strauss, and Japanese melodies. I can testify that letting students choose their own music is *not* a good idea—it just becomes reinforcement for off-task behavior.

- SIMON SAYS: Even Grade 9 students love this old game. To make it harder and more challenging, call it "Simon *doesn't* say" and have the responses the opposite of what the students are used to. Fun! Fun! Fun! Just don't forget the three Rs after the game is over!

- NAMES/NAMES/NAMES: Every school today has access to computers, and excellent crossword and word search programs are available. Make up both types of game, using the names of the students in your class. The word search is obvious. With the crossword, simply plug in the students' names as the answers, and then say something about each student to create the clues. For example, "Bobby" is the answer to "the one who always drops his books when he walks past Jenny's desk." Students *love* these, so be sure to set a five-minute time limit for the refocuser, then use the puzzles again as reinforcers.

- JOKES: Stop the class and ask if anyone has a good joke to share, making it clear the content must be suitable. Let three jokes be told, but in case no one volunteers, keep a joke, limerick or pun book handy. Joke books are available at any bookstore. Ones I like are Robert Orben's *Two Thousand Sure-Fire Jokes for Speakers and Writers* (Doubleday), *The Joke-Teller's Handbook or 1,999 Belly Laughs* (Wilshire) and *Twenty-Five Hundred Jokes to Start 'Em Laughing* (Wilshire). *The Random House Book of Jokes & Anecdotes*, edited by Joe Claro, is also good. Of course, the type of joke book you use will depend upon the age of your students; the aforementioned are more appropriate for upper elementary or Junior High. A few good joke books for younger students are *The Great All-Time Excuse Book* by Maureen Kushner, *The Craziest Riddle Book in the World* by Lori Miller Fox, and *Giggles, Gags & Groaners* by Joseph Rosenbloom, all published by Sterling. The monthly *Reader's Digest* is also an excellent source of jokes and anecdotes for all ages.

- WEIRD WORDS: These are those unusual configurations of words that involve the use of shape, space and imagination in order to deciper word meanings (see Appendix D). Stop your class, put a couple of these on the chalkboad or overhead, see who can figure them out first, then resume work with the three Rs.

- CARTOON TIME: Stop the class, turn on the overhead, and enjoy a couple of cartoon strips that are age and content appropriate for your students: *Hi and Lois* and *Peanuts* are good examples. You can base a cartoon file on the daily newspaper or even create your own cartoons as I have done.

- NAME ALLITERATIONS: Each student must introduce him/herself by adding an alliterative adjective before his or her name, for example, Beautiful Becky or Terrific Tom. The trick is to remember as many of the alliterations as possible. This activity does more than permit refocusing. It serves as a good memory trainer, too!

- THE UNEXPECTED: Call for something totally different, for example, students turning their desks to face the back of the room. The only rationale you need is that the class seems bored and restless and that by changing the pattern, they will all have a renewed sense of motivation. The switch, coupled with your positive approach, will work. You can also tell the students to work anywhere *except* at their desks! At first, they will not believe you, but this, too, can be effective. Once, while utilizing this ploy, I had students everywhere—on top of my filing cabinet, under my desk, behind curtains, in cupboards, on window ledges and lying all over the floor. The principal, accompanied by the area superintendent, decided to make a surprise visit. Although the students were all working, the situation must have caused considerable concern to my principal who tactfully mumbled, "Ms. Paterson has some rather different teaching techniques," and slipped out.

- WORD FUN: Stop the class, give them a word from the dictionary that you are sure they will not recognize, then, in pairs, have them attempt to define the word. Let them share some of their definitions, but watch the time—this activity is just a refocuser—and then give them the real definition. Making up meanings can have hilarious results and can become an entire lesson in itself, if the correct meaning is then discussed and entered in students' vocabulary books. I once used the word "vinegarroon," which refers to a large non-venomous, scorpion-like arachnid. Here are a few definitions coined by a Grade 7 class: a bridegroom who is tied up; gallons of wine; man-eating vines; a French barmaid (I have *no* idea where this came from!). Turn to a large dictionary such as *Webster's New World Dictionary, Third College Edition*, for word possibilities. See also Appendix E in this book.

- THE SILENCE CHALLENGE: This is one of the few activities that improves with use! The first time you try it, you stop the class by whatever method works for you and challenge your students (the key word is "challenge") to remain absolutely silent—not even a sneeze or cough is allowed—for as long as they can. I have never yet had a class make it past about 10 seconds on the first try. They will probably want to try again immediately, but refuse and act upon the three Rs. The *next* time you challenge the class to be silent, however, you will have their first time written on the board for all to see. Students love the idea of beating their own time, and get better and better at this. In addition to giving them a time out, this refocuser helps to calm everyone.

- THE BOX: Sometimes, for lack of any other refocusing ideas, I have dug into my special Box (see Chapter 2, pages 23-24) and retrieved something that caught my fancy. Once you have an object such as a shell, call attention to it and say you are going to brainstorm for all of its possible uses. Make it a male versus female challenge to get total co-operation. Keep score, set a time limit, and have students agree that ideas must make sense and be "clean" and that boys and girls will speak alternately without repeating what another has said. You can get a lot of mileage out of this idea, depending, of course, on what is in The Box. Prizes are up to you. (See Chapter 1, pages 16-17 for possibilities.)

- NOTHING TIME OUT: If your class is restless and unproductive, then tell them you can see their restlessness, and so are calling a nothing time out. For one to two minutes they are not allowed to do anything, including talking, moving and wiggling. The time span can be longer if necessary to reach the stage where you can see that the students are bursting to be active. Tell them that since doing nothing is so boring, then they might just as well get back to work. A few smart alecs will say they prefer to do nothing, but you cannot win them all!

- SILENT SCREAM: There are two ways to carry out this refocuser:

  1. Interrupt the class and ask everyone to try to yawn. Someone will, and as we well know, yawning is contagious. Try to get as many students yawning and stretching as possible—they will feel better for it. Then it is time for the three Rs.
  2. Tell students to imagine they are in a silent movie and are furiously screaming at someone or something. Let them use appropriate arm movements, but have them remain in their desks. This refocuser works in the same manner as No. 1 above.

- INDIVIDUAL REFOCUSING: When one or two individuals require refocusing, discover what is distracting them. Be open-minded about their responses and offer either common-sense advice or a bit of personal attention. For example, I once found a student preoccupied by what her thighs would look like in a swimsuit at an upcoming date. I suggested a rub-on tan cream which relieved her mind enough so that she could concentrate on her assignment.

- COMIC TIME OUT: I always keep an updated box of comics, magazines, joke books, and the like on hand. If the class as a whole is really off task, I sometimes resort to a five-minute comic time out. It has nothing whatsoever to do with the task at hand, as I readily admit to the students, but if students are off task anyway it sure does not hurt to try.

- STRETCH: Cue by asking students to stand *on* their chairs. (This gets attention quickly.) Of course, safety must be considered, but assuming that the chairs are low and sturdy, ask students to stretch their fingers by spreading them wide apart and then their arms by reaching up. Follow each stretch with "hold...relax." Or, have students stretch all muscles, one at a time, and end by saying, "On the count of 3, you will gently slip down into your desks, like pieces of melting wax, and as you sit, you harden into perfect students—ready to work!''

• RIDDLES: Riddles of any kind are fun for all and can be found in many children's books. What is the answer to this one?

> In marble walls as white as milk,
> Lined with a skin as soft as silk
> Within a fountain crystal clear,
> A golden apple doth appear,
> No doors there are to this stronghold,
> Yet things break in and steal the gold.
>
> (AN EGG)

Refocusers differ from anticipatory sets in that they may not relate to the lesson you are trying to teach. Nonetheless, they are valuable. They draw in the students' wandering attention and give you another opportunity to direct student energies to the lesson at hand. When refocusing, be sure to remember the importance of keeping good control of the class during the time out, of ensuring the activity lasts no more than five minutes, and of following it with reminding, reassuring and reinforcing. Above all, you must have confidence in the students' ability to return to the task at hand.

Chapter 9:   Closing the Lesson

Nothing is so difficult as a beginning...unless perhaps the end.

Lord Byron, Don Juan

A book on beginnings would be incomplete without some mention of endings. We teachers all know the importance of "closing" a lesson, of ending it in such a way that the students can store new information neatly away in their long-term memories. Nonetheless, our lessons sometimes fall short of the ideal. How familiar are the following scenarios to you?

- In the middle of your explanation of a very important idea, the bell rings and your room empties.
- You are just about to assign that night's homework and the bell cuts you off...no homework!
- A student who seldom talks is finally offering a well thought-out response...ring!
- About eight students are waiting for help at your desk...ring!
- You are just getting into the meat of your lesson, you have a captive audience and...ring! ring!

I have experienced all these situations more than once and wonder if all teachers must have nightmares about bells! Whether you have them or not, you can be sure when your lesson is interrupted, much of it will be lost.

The sports activity analogy that I introduced in Chapter 1 is relevant to lesson closings too. A good athlete would never perform without doing both a warm-up and an appropriate cool down. A good teacher needs the same discipline. I teach aerobics, which releases my stress from teaching Junior High, and frequently run out of time to effect a good close, in this case, a series of stretches. But I cannot go past the hour because I teach at a club with back-to-back classes. As a result, I find myself shouting at the backs of departing participants, "Stretch in the shower!" This desperate cry is about as effective as a teacher shouting to departing students, "Today we learned...."

Psychologists assure us that what we remember best is what we hear first and last. If you shout, "Pick up that mess..." as your students rush out the door, then that is what they will remember. We must be *time wise*, and plan as good a conclusion to each of our lessons as we did a beginning. A good "close" is what every salesperson aims for: teachers are salespersons of knowledge who need good closes, too. Here are a few rules to remember when considering that all-important ending to your lesson.

1. The close sould be a brief recalling of exactly what was done in that class. It can be provided either by the teacher ("Today we learned that fractions must have common denominators before they can be added...") or by a student ("Billy, please tell me what we learned today..."). *Key points only!*
2. Make the close at least five minutes before the bell rings so that some time for reflection is available. In fact, *insist* on a few seconds of silent thinking immediately after the close in order to encourage retention of the fact(s).
3. The same words that were used to close a class's last lesson in a subject should be used near the beginning of their next lesson in that subject. For example: "Yesterday we learned that to add or subtract fractions a common denominator is required. Today we will...." In other words, there is a definite link between set and conclusion.
4. You may find it appropriate to ask one student or more to paraphrase the close. We all know the value of such "relearning."

Allow me to "close" *Ready...Set...Teach!* In this book, I have emphasized the importance of providing anticipatory sets at the outset of some lessons and have made specific suggestions for sets by curriculum areas. In addition, I have discussed the importance of an appropriate lesson closure.

One other benefit of making a planned lesson closing is worth mentioning. When we make one, we are not only assisting our students in remembering what we have been trying to teach, but helping parents and children overcome the blank minds brought on by the familiar question, "What did you learn in school today?" By offering exact, succinct "closes" and having students repeat them back to us, we can improve the odds of students remembering information from that particular lesson. That means a student might actually have a reasonable answer for an inquiring parent. Can you imagine the surprise on the face of a parent who hears, "Today, we learned that for every action there is an equal and opposite reaction!"?

Teachers, however, are human. Although we may meet every morning with renewed enthusiasm and the best of plans to introduce both set and close, to treat all students with equal respect, not to lose our tempers and so on—we seldom accomplish as much as we would like to. Sometimes, at the end of a day, rather than recalling our accomplishments, we think back instead to the errors we have made, the time we have "lost." (How could time have so betrayed us?) There is no calling back the day, but luckily there is tomorrow! And we can try again, because teaching is learning, and to this there is no end—ever.

Chapter 10:   Putting Sets in Perspective

The test of a teacher's success is that the audience—the students—remain spellbound and find pleasure in their tasks.

K. Paterson

Let me remind you that the anticipatory set is only one small part of teaching. In *Ready...Set...Teach!* I have attempted to tear it apart and examine it from its simplest to most complicated forms. But I would like to repeat that creating a super set for every single lesson you teach would be impossible and impractical; overlooking the concept completely is equally impossible and impractical.

Many teachers working in a variety of subject areas already use anticipatory sets effectively. For example, one day as I was passing the open door to a Grade 9 Social Studies class, I could not help but note the absolute absence of noise from the room. I peeked in. There was the teacher, a conscientious, elderly man, standing *on* his desk, conducting a detailed lecture on a relatively boring topic. The students, however, were mesmerized. At another time, I saw a popular Physical Education and Science teacher, who usually dressed in ragged-looking sweat shorts and a tank top for the gym, don a beautiful, black blazer (over the aforementioned apparel) and stand erectly before his awestruck class. The students, usually an unruly lot, were fully attentive as he told them, in all seriousness, that the topic of the day's lesson, ozone layer destruction, was very grave indeed!

"But I'm not creative!" I often hear this from teachers, and my first response is, "Oh, but you are! Every teacher is! How else could you juggle 30 different personality types at once, just to mention one of the many responsibilities your job entails?" Then my second response is, "Necessity truly is the mother of invention, and necessity, therefore, breeds creativity!"

If you know you need a set but your mind keeps drawing a blank, try the following:

• Focus on what constitutes a good set.
• Recall your lesson objectives.
• Scan your special Box for ideas.
• If nothing comes to you, drop the idea. Something just might jump out of nowhere when you are least expecting it. My best sets have been created in hindsight (but I can then use them next time...), at 3 a.m. (hence, the writing pad by my bed), or when I am walking my dog. In fact, I had so many flashes of promptly forgotten creativity while dog walking that I invested in a small dictaphone that I now carry with me everywhere.

If you still have to teach that lesson without a good set, don't worry! You will captivate your students next time!

"But games like that only work with little kids" I also hear when I am vaunting the merits of the set. Not so! I was once one of more than 200 university students in a class taught by a tiny, insignificant-looking professor who never failed to keep everyone of us alert. Her sets were so magnificent that, as the term progressed, her mere entrance into the amphitheatre created silence. She always carried a large brown bag to class, and the bag's contents always amazed us. Some days she never even opened the bag, but it was there, nevertheless. Naturally, she became known to us as The Bag Lady, and we loved her! Once she turned her back for a second and donned a cardboard crown (which upon close examination looked as if it had been made by a grandchild). When she turned back to face us, her entire demeanor had changed, and we knew, even before she said "We are not amused," that she had become Queen Victoria. A few minutes later, she turned her back again, readjusted the same crown, changed her facial appearance and suddenly we saw Henry VIII before us. Her lesson lent itself to several such transformations and she kept her adult audience captivated for two hours! I rest my case!

Creating the perfect set may not always be possible—but neither is creating the perfect lesson. I merely ask that we, as teachers with captive audiences, be aware of the virtues, the rewards, and the worth of this simple teaching technique.

Not all of us need to resort to the theatrics involved in many of the sets suggested in this book. I admire those teachers whose very presence in a room commands attention and whose mere glances seem able to encourage even the most unmotivated students to focus. I, however, am not such a teacher, and I am continually faced with students who would rather be anywhere else but in my classroom. And somehow I believe I am not the only such teacher! It is for us—the teachers who require that little extra something to get our classes centred—that this book is written. As I suggested earlier, we are not *just* teachers, but also actors and entertainers. As actors, we will not get curtain calls; as entertainers, we will not get standing ovations; but as teacher-actor-entertainers, we *will* receive the incomparable satisfaction of knowing that at least a part of our lessons will be stored away in the dark recesses of some young minds, to be called forth when needed, to be remembered. And remember, if at first you do not succeed, if your sets are cumbersome and seem to be more trouble than they are worth, don't give up! Try a new approach, a different type of set tomorrow. Those who try most will fail most, but failure is delay—not defeat! And the students are worth the effort!

Appendix A: Students as Protagonists

I have successfully used this story form with grades 5 through 9; just be aware of whose name goes where! You need to know your students well before using this technique, so that you do not over-look any of them or innocently hurt any feelings. Casting students against type is funny only if the students see it that way. Be sure a student will; ask him or her ahead of time if you have any doubts. I typecast students as much as possible, but even then, knowing your students well is essential.

Wild Waters Adventure of (Class Name)

"I can hardly wait," _1_ shrieked happily.

"Me neither," added _2_. "This will be great."

_1_, the teacher of the 25 excited Grade _____ students who were anxiously waiting on the rocky edge of the angry-looking river looked considerably less pleased than her class. "Remember," she cautioned, "not all of us can swim. _3_, _4_, _5_ and _6_, you are all good swimmers, so please stay close to your buddies. And everyone remember to..."

"Oh, don't worry so much, _T_," laughed _7_. She was a cheerful girl who always saw the best in everything. "Nothing can happen."

"She's right! I mean, they wouldn't take us if it was, you know, dangerous or anything...would they?" asked _8_, a tiny girl who looked less enthusiastic than the others.

"Of course not!" _9_, one of the unspoken class leaders, said confidently.

"Look!" shouted _10_. "There they are now!" Sure enough, three large rubber dingy-type boats, steered by what appeared to be orange-suited aliens, were headed toward them. _T_ sighed. Ever since her class had won this river raft adventure in the (Name a newspaper) _____ Creative Writing Contest, she hadn't had a decent night's sleep. But soon, it would be over. She watched as the first orange alien docked his boat and removed his orange rubber hood to reveal a smiling young man underneath. "Hi kids!" he announced above the roar of the river. "You lucky guys are in for the ride of your lives! I'm Abe. These are Barney and James. We're your guides down the wild waters of the wonderful (Name a major river within a day's drive) _____ River. And let me tell you, what with this wind and all, she's pretty frisky today! Climb in...eight to a boat. Hey, teach! You can come with me!"

"O happy day," thought _T_ to herself, but she smiled and accepted Abe's outstretched hand. The craft was wobbly and certainly didn't feel safe, but then what did she know about river rafting?

"_T_," whispered _8_ as the girl huddled beside her teacher, "I'm kinda scared!"

"Not me," shouted _11_ as he bravely stood up in the dingy and gave a loud "whoopee" to the winds. _11_ was an athletic boy, known for his courage and charm, but this was no time for either as far as _11_ was concerned.

"Sit down, _11_," _T_ scolded, "and you too, _12_! Stop trailing your hand in the water. You're getting your sleeves wet!"

81

"Ah, teach, you'd better relax a bit," laughed Abe as he skillfully guided the tiny craft away from shore. "These kids are gonna get a lot more than their sleeves wet before this is over!"

"Yes!" shrieked _13_ from James's boat which was close beside at that moment. "Here we go!"

"Hang in you guys," said _14_ rather nervously. Already the dingies were rocking and twisting and the river, here, was relatively calm. _14_ was an intelligent, concerned girl who sometimes mothered the others. At the moment, she was looking a little green and not particularly happy. _15_, her best friend, was clinging to her sleeve, eyes wide and frightened.

Beside them, _16_, a quiet, sensitive boy, was holding his waterproof poncho tightly around him to fend off the spray from the other crafts. "I'm soaked already," he muttered.

"Yeah! Ain't it great!" laughed _12_. For a few moments the three small rubber dingies bounced and danced along the gentle bubbles and around the tiny rocks sticking out of the water, and the more nervous among the passengers began to relax.

"Maybe this won't be so bad after all," thought _17_ to herself. She hadn't wanted to come...had actually considered feigning illness today, but her friend, _18_, had insisted. She glanced at _18_. She certainly seemed to be enjoying herself. In fact, she was flirting with James, their orange alien captain!

Suddenly, however, a loud clap of thunder split the sky and, without warning, the skies opened, and torrents of rain pounded the helpless crafts below. For just the slightest of moments, Abe looked scared. But then he quickly signalled to the other two dingies to dock as soon as possible.

"No worries," he assured his passengers. "We know what we're doing. This happens all the time. Just hang on tight."

"Hang on to *what*?" shouted _19_. "Everything's slippery!"

"Here, hold on to me, and I'll hold on to _20_," suggested _21_ as he tried valiantly to remain calm.

_T_ could contain herself no longer. "Now see here, young

man. This has become altogether too dangerous! Take us back immediately!''

Abe looked at _11_ and shouted, ''Can you keep her quiet? We're doin' the best we can!'' _11_ nodded and moved carefully to sit beside his distraught teacher.

''Don't worry,'' he said to her, but his voice was unconvincing, ''I'm sure that—''

His words were cut off by screams. The water had become a churning mass as rocks and rapids rose viciously out of the rain.

The third dingy, containing _17_, _18_, _22_, _23_, _24_, _25_, _9_ and Barney had capsized, spewing its unsuspecting passengers into the violent undercurrent.

''Help!'' screamed _17_ as she clawed vainly at the foaming surges around her, ''I can't swim!'' Instantly _9_ was at her side, his arm around her neck. He had her, but where was he to take her? He could see nothing but mist and wild water. Suddenly, an enormous tree root emerged in front of him and he grabbed at it with every ounce of strength he could muster. He had it! Painfully he clung to the precious root, and dragged _17_'s limp body across it. Now what?

Meanwhile, Abe had managed to dock his craft and was charging back into the roaring waters, _11_ and _13_ courageously at his side, to help pull in James's craft.

_7_, _14_ and _18_ were shuddering violently as the boys helped them to shore. There the little group slowly grew, huddled together, waiting, watching, for the others.

''They're dead! I *knew* we should never have come on this stupid trip!'' shouted _14_ hysterically. _24_ patted her hand gently, but said nothing.

''Isn't there anything we can do?'' sobbed _18_. Her best friend _17_ was out there somewhere, in the icy water—missing.

Suddenly the third dingy, or what was left of it, flew onto the shore on the back of a monstrous wave. It was badly torn and shredded. One look at it and _23_ and _24_ began to cry too.

''I can't believe this!'' whispered _24_. ''I can't believe this!''

"Let's go out there and find them! Let's help Abe and James!" shouted _12_, his courage renewed by anger at the thought of his friends drowning and him doing nothing.

"*No!*" shouted _T_, but her authority was gone as _12_, _5_ and _6_ formed a chain by linking arms and started into the river.

The watchers on shore were frozen with fear! Anxiously, they peered into the thick mist, and saw nothing. Again and again they called names and heard nothing except the rumbling of the thunder and howling of the river. Time stood still. They waited.

Then—there they were!—a soaked group of survivors dragging one another towards shore a few metres downstream. The kids on shore rushed to meet them, to help, to carry, to support, to offer encouragement. Abe had _10_ over his shoulder and his other arm around _14_. Barney was carrying _15_ because she had broken her ankle. James was being helped by _16_ and _19_ because his head was bleeding and he seemed to be almost unconscious. Instantly, everyone took action. _4_ began applying pressure to James's head. _1_ and _2_ took _15_ from Barney and tried to make her comfortable. There were hugs and tears of joy everywhere until suddenly _18_ screamed, "Where's _9_ and _17_?"

"And _17_ can't swim," whispered _18_.

"Oh no," cried _T_ as she hurried again to the edge of the water. It was raining so hard now that seeing where the river began and the shore ended was impossible.

"Lady, we can't do nothing now," Abe said earnestly. "Best we get these kids back to somewhere warm, and send out search parties with lights. It's too dark. Can't see nothing out there!"

"I can't leave them," _T_ cried.

"No choice," added Barney as he and Abe forcefully pulled _T_ away from the wild waters.

The exhausted group that sat around the fire, huddled in blankets and sipping on hot chocolate, was absolutely silent. In every mind was the same thought. _9_ and _17_ were gone—dead! But no one dared speak the words aloud. The waiting was almost intolerable. The hysterical crying had changed to gentle sobbing, to silence. And they waited! And waited! Hundreds of well-equipped rescuers were scouting the area, but that was no consolation! The waiting... the "not knowing" was driving them all crazy.

Just when they were sure they couldn't take another moment of the terrible waiting, the doors burst open and three burly men pushed in with _9_ and _17_ in their arms. _9_ was conscious and he offered a weak smile at the others as they cheered in excited unison. _17_, however, was limp and silent in the big man's arms.

_18_ rushed up to him, "Is she...is she...?"

"She's gonna be OK, little lady. Just needs to thaw out a bit. She's gonna be fine—thanks to this young fella here. He saved her life. Must have clung to that root for a good three hours with an unconscious girl in his other arm. Amazing! Absolutely amazing!"

The cheer that went up from the others was deafening! They mobbed _9_, everyone wanting to get a peek at their new hero. Suddenly all fear was forgotten in the rush of excitement of finding everyone safe after all.

"I always knew we'd come through this," _11_ said loudly.

"Yeah, me too," added _12_. "I mean, what sort of a class would we be if we let a little water break us up!"

"And you were worried, _8_, when we have guys with egos as big as this in our group?" laughed _14_.

_7_ smiled, and her eyes gazed with a new respect upon her class.

"You have all been wonderful! You have proved that you can handle any emergency! I am proud of you. But," and she emphasized this with a long silence, "our *next* field trip is going to be to the...library!"

M – male   F – female   X – either

Add the names to the appropriate numbers in the story.

TEACHER T_____

1. X_____		14. F_____
2. X_____		15. F_____
3. X_____		16. M_____
4. X_____		17. F_____
5. X_____		18. F_____
6. X_____		19. M_____
7. F_____		20. X_____
8. F_____		21. M_____
9. M_____		22. X_____
10. M_____		23. F_____
11. M_____		24. F_____
12. M_____		25. X_____
13. X_____		

Consider some of the following uses for this story:

1. Comprehension questions
2. Intuitive questions (What happens next?)
3. Sequencing strategies
4. Grammar activities: parts of speech; figures of speech such as similes; tenses; sentence structures; use of dialogue; punctuation
5. Story parts
6. Character analysis
7. Types of writings: descriptive, narrative, etc.
8. "What if" questions
9. Writing activities: thank-you letters to the river raft company; a sequel to the story; a description of the river, the rafts, the rescuers, the destroyed dingy...; a newspaper article on the story; a report of the incident for parents; a poem about the adventure
10. Stimulus for illustrations about some part of the story

Appendix B: Playing with Parts of Speech

Ask the students to supply you with nouns, verbs, adjectives and adverbs as needed for your sentences with blanks. List their words in sequence on the chalkboard, then read the sentences on an overhead, filling in the appropriate blanks with the students' words. Sometimes these work wonderfully; sometimes a little teacher assistance is required to elicit an appropriate word.

Note: Where there is a centred horizontal line (——), put the name of one of the students in the room. Doing so adds further motivation to the exercise. Use your own name in the teacher (T) blanks.

1: Nouns

• Yesterday —— drove home in a __1__ and ate __2__ for dinner.

• —— got stuck in ——'s __3__ .

• A huge __4__ gave —— a __5__ .

• ——'s favorite thing in the world is __6__ .

• —— gave —— a beautiful __7__ for being such a good __8__ .

2: Verbs

Depending on the level of students' knowledge, indicate the tense required or simply choose that tense yourself.

- ⸺ had to hurry and _1_ so he could _2_ to the party.
- ⸺ _3_ ed and _4_ ed when ⸺ _5_ ed.
- In ⸺'s dream a dinosaur _6_ and _7_.
- ⸺ and ⸺ were _8_ ing together.
- _7_ told the class to _9_ and _10_ before the bell _11_.

3: Adjectives and Adverbs (*)

- The _1_, _2_ animal jumped at ⸺.
- ⸺ likes _3_ girls/boys who talk _4*_.
- For lunch ⸺ had a _5_ sandwich which he/she ate _6*_.
- ⸺ runs but ⸺ runs _7*_ because he/she is _8_ er.
- Our _9_ school is _10_ because we have _11_ teachers, and we all work _12*_.

4: Parts of Speech in Paragraphs

Homework is not _1_ but it is necessary. The best place to do it is in/on a _2_ after you have eaten a _3_ supper of _4_ and _5_. Sit _6_ and try to _7_. Work _8_ and _9_. If you feel _10_, _11_ close your eyes a few times to try to get rid of the feeling. If this does not work, _12_ around _13_ and _14_ _15_.

This might help, or it might just cause your _16_ parents to think you have gone insane. Either way, it will help you to get all your _17_ homework done.

1. adjective	7. verb	13. adverb
2. noun	8. adverb	14. verb
3. adjective	9. adverb	15. adverb
4. noun	10. adjective	16. adjective
5. noun	11. adverb	17. adjective
6. adverb	12. verb	

Never take a __1__ to school. If you do, your __2__ teacher will surely __3__. He/she will turn __4__ and start to __5__ and __6__. Then he/she will ask you to please remove the __7__, but you won't be able to because you will be __8__ing too hard. Your teacher might pick up a __9__ __10__ and throw it at the __11__. Then you really have trouble, because no doubt the principal will __12__ on the scene, __13__ing and __14__ing. What can you do then? __15__ quickly and head for __16__.

1. noun
2. adjective
3. verb
4. adverb
5. verb
6. verb

7. (same as No. 1)
8. verb
9. adjective
10. noun
11. (same as No. 1)

12. verb
13. verb
14. verb
15. verb
16. noun

Appendix C: Math Chuckles

TEACHER: A banana truck weighed 1 t, the bananas weighed 1591 kg, and the first man on the truck weighed 73 kg. What did the second man weigh?
STUDENT: I don't know.
TEACHER: He weighed the bananas!
Lesson: Problem solving using operations

TEACHER: I'm making metric cookies.
STUDENT: What are you going to call them?
TEACHER: Gram crackers!
Lesson: Introduction to metric system

DAD: What are you studying in school these days?
STUDENT: Mostly GOZINTA, Dad.
DAD: What's GOZINTA? A new foreign language?
STUDENT: No, just GOZINTA. 2 GOZINTA 4, 2 times; 4 GOZINTA 8, 2 times...
Lesson: Long division

TEACHER: If I had a beef steak and cut it in two, what would I get?
STUDENT: Quarters.

TEACHER: Then if I cut it again?

STUDENT: Eighths.

TEACHER: Correct, and if I cut it again?

STUDENT: Sixteenths.

TEACHER: Yes! And again?

STUDENT: Hamburger!

Lesson: Introduction to fractions and decimals

TEACHER: If there are four sheep, two dogs, and one herdsman, how many feet are there altogether?

STUDENT: Twenty-six?

TEACHER: No! Sheep have hooves; dogs have paws and so there are just the two feet of the herdsman.

Lesson: Problem solving—dealing with irrelevant data

TEACHER: Seven cows were in a single line. Which one turned around and said, "I see four pairs of horns?"

STUDENT: The third cow?

TEACHER: Nope! Cows can't talk!

Lesson: Problem solving—how to use diagrams to help do it

TEACHER: What do you call it if nine elephants wear pink sneakers and one wears blue?

STUDENT: Stupid?

TEACHER: Nine out of 10 elephants prefer pink; ratio 9:1.

Lesson: Introduction to ratios

Define a circle.

...A round line with no kinks in it, joined up so as not to show where it began.

Lesson: Geometry

Note: When using a math chuckle such as any of the above, identify yourself as the teacher and choose the name of one of your students for student lines.

Appendix D: Weird Words and Phrases

Most of these were created by one of my Grade 7 Language Arts classes. You may well wish to invite your students to do this activity too. In the meantime, you can use the following as refocusers.

Too wise you are.	Y Y U R
Too wise you be.	Y Y U B
I see you are.	I C U R
Too wise for me!	Y Y 4 ME
'Em are bugs!	M R (bugs)
'Em are not bugs!	MR NOT (bugs)
Oh yes they are!	O S A R
See de iddy biddy eyes?	C D E D B D iii's ?
Underachiever	achiever / under
Broken Heart	(broken heart symbol)

Clue	Rebus
Dark Thoughts	**THOUGHTS**
Crying Eyes	ʲʲʲʲʲʲ ° ° ° °
Light Switch	Switch
Afterthought	thought after
Scrambled Eggs	gseggesg
Rough Seas	CCCC
I See You	ICU
Underwear	wear / under
Look Behind You	U LOOK
Heavy Hand	**HAND**
Sidewalk	walk (sideways)
Broken Leg	L E G
Square Root	ROOT
Overtime	OVER / TIME
Double Shift	shiftshift
Upside Down	updown (upside down)
Reverse Gear	RAEG
Skinnydipping	dipping
Breakfast	FAST
Mixed Up	UP UP (jumbled)
Man Overboard	man / board

Appendix E: Big Word Fun

Here are some words with which to help your students refocus. Students must guess the meaning of the word you choose without referring to a dictionary. Only after they have done so do you provide the real meaning.

Bubo (noun) an inflammatory swelling of a lymph gland
Dottle (noun) unburned or partially burned tobacco in the bowl of a pipe
Epochal (adjective) uniquely or highly scientific
Ersatz (adjective) being an artificial or inferior substitute
Forbye (adjective) in addition; besides
Frugivorous (adjective) feeding on fruit
Harupsication (noun) any act of foretelling something
Helve (noun) a handle of a tool or weapon
Natatorium (noun) an indoor swimming pool
Ootheca (noun) a firm-walled egg case (as of a cockroach)
Pteridoid (adjective) related to or resembling a fern
Rhinolaryngology (noun) a branch of medicine dealing with the nose and larynx
Rive (verb) to wrench or tear apart
Strobilus (noun) twisted object, pinecone
Varus (adjective) knock-kneed
Yawp (verb) to make a raucous noise, to clamor, to complain

Index